IMPROVING LIBRARY INSTRUCTION:
HOW TO TEACH AND HOW TO EVALUATE

Papers Presented at the Eighth Annual Conference
on Library Orientation for Academic Libraries
held at Eastern Michigan University, May 4-5, 1978

edited by
Carolyn A. Kirkendall
Director, Project LOEX
Center of Educational Resources
Eastern Michigan University

Published for the
Center of Educational Resources,
Eastern Michigan University
by

Pierian Press
ANN ARBOR, MICHIGAN
1979

Library of Congress Catalog Card No. 79-87707
ISBN 0-87650-109-9

Z
711.2
.L47x
no. 9

Copyright © 1979, The Pierian Press
All Rights Reserved

PIERIAN PRESS
P.O. Box 1808
Ann Arbor, Michigan 48106

IMPROVING LIBRARY INSTRUCTION

LIBRARY ORIENTATION SERIES

Number one: LIBRARY ORIENTATION: Papers Presented at the First Annual Conference on Library Orientation held at Eastern Michigan University, May 7, 1971

Number two: A CHALLENGE FOR ACADEMIC LIBRARIES: How to Motivate Students to Use the Library (Papers Presented at the Second Annual Conference on Library Orientation for Academic Libraries, Eastern Michigan University, May 4-5, 1972)

Number three: PLANNING AND DEVELOPING A LIBRARY ORIENTATION PROGRAM; Proceedings of the Third Annual Conference on Library Orientation for Academic Libraries (Eastern Michigan University, May 3-4, 1973)

Number four: EVALUATING LIBRARY USE INSTRUCTION: Papers Presented at the University of Denver Conference on the Evaluation of Library Use Instruction, December 13-14, 1973

Number five: ACADEMIC LIBRARY INSTRUCTION; OBJECTIVES, PROGRAMS, AND FACULTY INVOLVEMENT. Papers of the Fourth Annual Conference on Library Orientation for Academic Libraries, Eastern Michigan University, May 9-11, 1974

Number six: FACULTY INVOLVEMENT IN LIBRARY INSTRUCTION; Their Views on Participation in and Support of Academic Library Use Instruction (Papers and Summaries from the Fifth Annual Conference on Library Orientation for Academic Libraries held at Eastern Michigan University, May 15-17, 1975)

Number seven: LIBRARY INSTRUCTION IN THE SEVENTIES: STATE OF THE ART; Papers Presented at the Sixth Annual Conference on Library Orientation for Academic Libraries held at Eastern Michigan University, May 13-14, 1976

Number eight: PUTTING INSTRUCTION IN ITS PLACE: IN THE LIBRARY AND IN THE LIBRARY SCHOOL; Papers Presented at the Seventh Annual Conference on Library Orientation for Academic Libraries held at Eastern Michigan University, May 12-13, 1977

Number nine: IMPROVING LIBRARY INSTRUCTION: HOW TO TEACH AND HOW TO EVALUATE; Papers Presented at the Eighth Annual Conference on Library Orientation for Academic Libraries held at Eastern Michigan University, May 4-5, 1978

Contents

Preface .... page vii
        Carolyn A. Kirkendall

Introduction to the Conference .... page ix
        Fred A. Blum

Perspectives On Learning and Motivation .... page 1
        Israel Woronoff

Instructional Development in Library Use Education ...... page 11
        Larry Hardesty

**Teaching the Librarian to Teach: The Situation
    in Britain** .... page 37
        Peter K. Fox

Project LOEX and the National Scene .... page 61
        Carolyn A. Kirkendall

Implementing Instructional Methods: A Panel .... page 65
        Katherine Rottsolk, Moderator

    The Freshman Instruction Program .... page 69
        Melissa Cain

    **Latent Image Technology for Feedback in
    Library Instruction** .... page 77
        John R. Lincoln

    Library Instruction With Slides and Slide/Tapes ...... page 83
        Judith L. Violette

**Library Instruction: Some Observations From the Past
and Some Questions About the Future** .... page 89
        Edward G. Holley

Evaluating Library Instrcution Programs: Three Experiences

    Effects of Evaulation on Teaching Methods .... page 97
        Mignon Adams

    Evaluating Student Knowledge of Facilities .... page 101
        Elizabeth Frick

    Evaluation as a Tool for Program Development ..... page 107
        Peter P. Olevnik

**Library Orientation and Instruction – 1977: An
Annotated Review of the Literature** .... page 113
        Hannelore B. Rader

List of Participants .... page 131

Preface

Carolyn A. Kirkendall
Director, Project LOEX

The Eighth Annual Conference on Library Orientation for Academic Libraries was held May 4 & 5, 1978, at Eastern Michigan University. This annual program is still labeled an "orientation" meeting. By now, however, most librarians prefer to use terms such as "bibliographic instruction" or "user education" to connote any sort of library use teaching activity more advanced than the conducted tour, and the Conferences certainly have addressed issues and topics more sophisticated than basic orientation practices. For the sake of unity, however, the Conferences will remain "orientation" meetings -- in title only.

Titling a conference in its planning stages can be somewhat chanceful. One hopes that the speakers and presentations in final form will match the name of the advertised program. This year's session was called "Improving Instruction, Then Proving its Worth: How to Teach and How to Evaluate," and was intended to serve as an introductory level conference on the basics of learning and teaching methodology and the basics of testing the effectiveness of teaching the use of the library. Through theoretical and practical presentations, both issues were addressed. This publication contains the speeches in order as presented.

Readers of these Proceedings should also keep in mind that participants at the annual Library Orientation meetings are not asked to present prepared papers, but to make speeches. Some speeches are easy to read, some easier to listen to. As these series of Proceedings are reports of presentations initially intended to be heard, they may vary in readability. Small group discussions provided the opportunity to informally consider workable methods and materials to implement basic learning theory and to discuss the areas and solutions to assess these methods.

Participants were hosted at a cocktail party by Pierian Press. The LOEX office and all Conference attendees are annually grateful to the people at Pierian for providing this occasion to informally meet with other practicing instruction librarians.

Special appreciation for assisting in Conference activities goes to the major speakers and to the discussion leaders who volunteered to share their expertise, to the staff of EMU's McKenny Union, and particularly to the LOEX secretary, Michelle Barnes.

INTRODUCTION TO THE EIGHTH ANNUAL CONFERENCE
on
LIBRARY ORIENTATION

Fred Blum
Director, Center of Educational Resources
Eastern Michigan University

It has been my privilege to welcome the conference participants on behalf of the Center of Educational Resources during the last few years, and I'm glad to have that opportunity again.

This year, there are some 190 librarians among you, from 36 states, the District of Columbia, Puerto Rico, three Canadian provinces, and England. Most of you are from university libraries, but many colleges, ten community colleges, and several medical and health science libraries are also represented.

Many of your institutions are Project LOEX members. I'm pleased to tell you that Project LOEX membership is growing. We are optimistic about continuation after Council on Library Resources grant support expires.

Project LOEX's special collection of materials bearing on library orientation and instruction is an important tool for academic libraries. This representative circulating collection includes such things as library skills workbooks, course outlines, successful LSEP grant proposals, program descriptions and objectives, and annual reports.

Project LOEX exhibits are in great demand; nine exhibits were provided to library conferences in the last five weeks.

The lively Project LOEX office, so ably administered by Project Director Carolyn Kirkendall, has experienced no lull in requests for information, materials, research and referral.

Last year I said that library instruction was one of the "growth" fields in librarianship. That remains true today, when there are few other growth areas.

Here at Eastern Michigan University it is also a growth field. For example, in the near future we hope to be able to announce a major grant to develop, implement and evaluate a program of library instruction for non--traditional students.*

I hope you will find this conference an enjoyable and rewarding experience. Apparently some of you have in the past; I see many returnees among you.

For this year's conference, we've brought together a number of specialists from academic libraries here and abroad, from EMU's Educational Psychology Department, and from the University of Michigan's Evaluating and Testing Service. We hope this will give you some new insights on library instruction from inside and outside the library profession. We're especially pleased that Dean Ed Holley of the University of North Carolina's School of Library Science will be able to join us later today. He will give the luncheon address tomorrow on "Library Instruction: Some Observations on the Past and Some Questions About the Future."

I know you have a full schedule ahead of you, so I'll wish you an enjoyable and rewarding conference, and let you get on with your agenda.

Have a good conference!

---

*This grant, under HEW's Library Research and Demonstration Program, has since been announced. Entitled "Library Services for Non--Traditional Students," it seeks to identify student attitudes and needs with respect to the academic library and to develop, implement, and evaluate a program of library service and instruction for students who have returned to formal education after some years out of school.

PERSPECTIVES ON LEARNING AND MOTIVATION

Israel Woronoff
Educational Psychology Department
Eastern Michigan University

We are here this morning to talk about learning theory. For some of you, this may be a review. For others, it may be new material. Basically, it will be information that everyone should have who is involved in the orientation process.

I'm going to define learning as simply a change in behavior as a result of experience. There are several different types of learning, and the first and simplest kind is called association. This is a very, very old principle of learning, and it's probably still the most common and most effective one in terms of an individual being able to retain information.

It is based on the association principle. When A is associated with B over a period of time, if A is called to mind, B automatically follows. In other words, if you think of needles, what's the next thing you think of? Pins. If you think of smoke, what do you think of? Fire. The basic idea is the principle of association, which is the simplest form of learning.

The second form of learning is the classical conditioning situation. You are all familiar with Pavlov's dog. This classical conditioning situation falls under the behaviorism school of learning. With classical conditioning, no motivation is necessary.

In Pavlov's case, when he presented meat to a dog, he noticed the response was salivation. When he then used a bell before the meat was presented, it did not cause salivation at first. About the tenth time the bell was rung and then the meat presented, the bell itself caused salivation. The meat is what is called the unconditioned stimulus, the salivation is the unconditioned response, while the bell is known as the conditioned stimulus. When the bell produces salivation, the latter is called the conditioned response. This should be an old review for many of you.

Now we go on to operant conditioning, which is a little more important. The reason it is more important is because we give it a lot more publicity. In the operant conditioning situation, we introduce a concept that's very important. And that concept is one which we find very frequently in library work, that of trial and error.

A trial and error situation is one in which the individual gives a response to a stimulus. The stimulus could be anything. For example, the individual walks in the library and wants to find out, without asking the assistance of a librarian, where the history section is. As he wanders through the library, he is going through the process of trial and error. Nope, that's the janitor's closet, that's the audio-visual section, and so on. When he eventually and accidentally hits upon a shelf of books about the Napoleonic era, he has reached his goal, and discovered the history section through trial and error.

When you achieve the goal you are after, in this case the history section, you will remember its location next time. The idea is that the response that is reinforced is the one that is maintained, and that is the basis of operant conditioning. You receive reinforcement or reward when you make the correct response. The result is that the response that you have given is the one which you will keep, the one you will repeat. This trial and error situation eventually becomes smoothed out so that over a period of time you will make the correct move. In other words, as you go into the library, you will find the thing you want by trial and error -- eventually.

Now, in operant conditioning, you have another facet that is very important. That is motivation. Motivation is not important in the association situation, but it becomes terribly important here.

What is motivation? Motivation is actually a drive and a goal. An individual who is motivated has to have some drive. And he must have a goal which he seeks.

This drive can be of two types, the primary drive and the secondary drive. The primary drive is biological in nature. If an individual seeks a necessity, something without which he will die, he's highly motivated. Primary drives have to do with, for example, hunger.

Skinner did a great deal of his work utilizing the hunger drive, by teaching pigeons, in effect, to play ping pong. By withholding the pigeons' feed until they became very hungry, Skinner taught his subjects to make appropriate moves to receive food. If the pigeon made an appropriate move of his beak toward a ping pong ball, his action was rewarded and his hunger satisfied. By rewarding the pigeon, the bird learns to make the proper moves. Through this action, this series of experiments dealing with the success of approximations, the birds learned to hit the ping pong ball first, as they were the first fed. The poor bird that let the ping pong ball go by was not rewarded, and went hungry.

This experiment was quite successful, to a point. It became a more complex matter when pigs were introduced as the subjects of the experiment. Using food as the mechanism, again, pigs were trained to drop wooden coin objects into slots of a wooden human figure -- a "people bank." For about two weeks, the pigs quite successfully performed the experiment and were rewarded for their performance. Surprisingly, after a couple of weeks, the pigs refused to continue this activity, which taught us something. It taught us that the behavioristic explanation of things just goes so far with complex nervous systems. Animals, having increasingly complex nervous systems, do not continue to respond to conditioning over a long period of time.

There are several other principles that I also want to mention. Among those which are particularly useful for the purposes of library people are the concepts of generalization and discrimination. The concept of generalization involves developing a similar response to similar stimuli.

What do we mean by that? For example, the letter "A" can be written in several alphabet forms. If the symbol approximately resembles the shape of an "A," we generalize and assume it is indeed an "A." The problem of generalization, however, is that you have to know when to generalize and when to discriminate.

Discrimination is the other side of the coin. With discrimination, similar stimuli are used to develop different responses. In terms of issues related to the library, can you see problems now developing?

Two other concepts to address as well, in relation to the latter topic, are the transfer of training and the element of practice.

A number of assumptions are made when you teach somebody something. You assume that when you teach somebody something, it will transfer to another situation. If you teach an individual to swing at a tennis ball with a tennis racquet, will you assume that the next time he has an object in his hand that is used to strike something, he will transfer the same swing? What if the objects are a baseball bat and a baseball? You will say, well -- obviously not. When I take a tennis racquet and I swing it against a tennis ball, I am utilizing a principle which is not the same principle that I'm transferring to taking a baseball bat and swinging it against a baseball.

The point is that if you do not teach for transfer, it will generally not occur. One must teach for transfer. A more glaring example of this principle is this. Are there are humanities librarians in the audience? The humanities are a series of subjects. Why are they named "humanities?" The basic idea of naming the subjects associated with humanities is that, if you study them, they will make you humane. It follows that if you study the liberal arts, you will become a liberal artist, or you will become liberal. Now you see the point of transfer: it doesn't occur.

Studying humanities does not, as far as we have any evidence to indicate, make you humane. Studying the liberal arts does not make you liberal, nor does it make you an artist. But the assumption under which these subjects were originally taught was that that is exactly what they would do. The transfer of training research indicates clearly that this does not occur.

Another point is this: you may have heard of the concept that "If I do this, it will make me think clearly, or logically." The concept of, for example: teaching geometry to students makes them think logically because there's a great deal of mathematical logic involved in geometry. Therefore, if I am to learn the axioms and theorems, and I learn how to develop and approve them, I am learning those things necessary to make me think logically. Unfortunately, it doesn't work. There are many people who know geometry who cannot transfer past the mathematics of it.

Here's another good example of this. I have a dear friend who's a mathematician. In terms of thinking logically in relation to mathematics, he is excellent. But we got into an argument the other night over some events in the news of the day, and I asked him why he took the position he did. He said, "I read it in the newspaper." And I said, "Now, you read a mathematical journal and you are very critical of the opinions in some of the articles. And yet you don't apply the same degree of criticism when you read the daily newspaper." And he had to agree with me. And hasn't spoken to me since. Transfer of training is one of those things that trick us. When you are teaching for transfer, you must show exactly and precisely how you are going to use it in the expected situation. It will remain in a vacuum if you do not.

With the element of practice, the assumption is that practice helps. I'm sure many of you believe this. How many of you think that practicing something makes it improve, that practice is excellent for learning something? Every single one of you! People really believe that practice helps. But practice by itself does not. You can practice the wrong thing over and over again, and all you have done is a tremendous job of mislearning something.

Practice has to be performed in terms of a specific reinforcement so that you know you are practicing accurately. It's only accurate practice that's functional. Practice is effective if performed with a guide, a cue to indicate whether you're practicing correctly or incorrectly.

Another entirely different system of learning is the Gestalt method. The Gestalt system is not based on the behavior of the stimulus response. For behaviorism, by the way, no mind is necessary. Have I mentioned anything previously about reasoning? About thinking? There is no such thing as thinking to a behaviorist.

The Gestalt proponents look at learning from a different perspective entirely. The Gestalts insist that people have minds. What does that mean? It means that we do not respond to a single stimulus, but to a pattern of stimuli. A stimulus is only understood in relation to a pattern, and the pattern is recognized by the organism, you -- the thinker. Once this perception of pattern takes place, then behavior occurs.

If the organism perceives the pattern incorrectly, he will behave incorrectly. If he perceives a pattern in a certain way, he will behave in accordance with his perception. When you are instructing in the library, you have to watch for the student's perception of the pattern that you are presenting. He, the student, will then behave accordingly. If he perceives a different pattern than you are transmitting, he will behave differently than you expect.

This is the Gestalt approach. See the difference? This latter school of thought involves thinking and reasoning.

Thinking is how we understand something. If you have never seen a tiger, and you want someone to describe a tiger to you, how are they going to be able to do it? By finding something in your experience that is similar to a tiger. Maybe a little pussycat. If a person is familiar with a cat, and can imagine it seven times larger, with stripes, and with claws enlarged accordingly, then he can understand what a tiger looks like. What the Gestalts are saying is that understanding comes from utilizing patterns into familiar experiences. What we've retained from our past experience and memory becomes important. You see the difference; the approach is extremely different, and, I think, has a great deal of possible fruitfulness for people in library work. Look at it from the pattern perspective.

There is another element and that is insight. Insight differs from trial and error. The original work on insight was done by a man who developed a series of experiments to find out what insight was. He used chimpanzees who were given different degrees of experience. One chimpanzee was given no experience; he was put in a room with a 17--foot ceiling and had some bananas strung from a stalk from the top of the ceiling which he could not reach. He was given a series of sticks and what the poor chimp proceeded to do was to take these sticks and throw them at the bananas, trying to knock the bananas down. That was the lowest level, the lowest level chimp.

The next chimp was given the experience of watching a human being take sticks and screw them together. These sticks fit into one another; they could be inserted and screwed together. This chimp was put in the same situation and, accordingly, when he got into that situation, and the sticks were distributed around the room, he gathered up the sticks, screwed them together and then proceeded to climb the stick to get the bananas. Of course, he fell down. But he would have eventually been able to balance himself to get a couple of bananas.

The third chimp was given the opportunity to observe a human being screw sticks together and then use the sticks to gather something with it, to use it: to knock something down. This chimp, under the same circumstances, when in the same situation, took the sticks, screwed them together, took the long stick and knocked the bananas down. A perfect example of what is called insight, as differing from trial and error. With the idea of insight you utilize your past experience for the purposes of solving a new situation. And this is extremely valuable.

If you can teach students to utilize their past experience into a new situation by seeing the similarity between the old situation and the new one, you've got insight working. And insight is a very, very, good basis for functioning.

Have you noticed the difference between insight and trial and error now? In trial and error, you are working in the dark and if by accident you get the thing right, you still don't know what you did right. You still have to come back and do it a few more times until it becomes something that is automatic. With insight, you are teaching people to utilize their past experience for the purposes of providing a resolution to a new problem.

Now I would like to return to motivation. Because motivation again is quite different. Remember that I mentioned that motivation consists of a drive and a goal, and I mentioned the primary drives? The primary drives are the drives which have to do with survival. You know, if you think of a primary drive you are thinking of hunger, you're thinking of thirst, you're thinking of temperature balance, when the temperature is equivalent to the body so that you cannot freeze to death or burn up with heat. We're thinking of things of that nature. These are what we classify as primary drives. Secondary drives are the ones that you can use most often. You cannot starve the students; you can send them dormitory food but you cannot starve them.

Our basis, then, has to be on the secondary drive principle. And with secondary drive you find yourself dealing with something else. Secondary drives are very powerful drives also. They have to do with social drives. People will perhaps go without food sometimes to look nice. That would be an example of the secondary drive. Secondary drive then has to do with appearance, has to do with social status, has to do with friendship, has to do with mastery: to do something well. People will want to attempt to do something well, so you have secondary drives in operation.

What librarians and other teachers can use are predominately the secondary drives, and this we have to make very good use of. Now I'm doing something that is very bad, by standing up here and lecturing to you this early in the morning. I notice a couple of you are still digesting your breakfast, a number of you are still involved in trying to get over last night's lack of sleep from being in a new place, and the result is that this form of learning is highly ineffective. It depends to a large extent on your personal motivation. And, we can't count on that. The worst thing in the world is to lecture to people, because they do the least amount of learning under these circumstances. If I had a light attached to each one of your heads which blinked every time you got distracted while I was talking, it would be awful! I would get off the platform immediately because there would be a light going on here, ten lights going off over there. I've been watching those ten lights there and then three lights over here, and so forth, so that the continual flashing on and off according to your attention span would be tremendous. Now, that's highly inefficient learning. Terribly inefficient.

There are other ways to do things. I'll give you an example. The Army used a very inefficient method when I was in the service during World War II. They used to threaten you with death and say: you will die if you don't know this. And after awhile, who cared? That's what it amounted to. It was really overused. There are much more imaginative systems. The Navy was much smarter. I wasn't in the Navy, so I can say that. The fact is the Navy hired educational psychologists to work on routines which would help them to learn more effectively. And the ways utilized were very, very clever indeed. Example: they set aside several months for the educational psychologist consultants to study the activities of boot camp.

When you're new in a boot camp, you try to get orientation. Like beginning to use the library, like library orientation. Now in the boot camp those in command found that by watching what was going on, they had the insight as to what the most effective learning processes could be. They found that the lectures that the Navy personnel gave were totally ineffective. And the fact was that they were dealing with very expensive equipment. Planes, battleships, things like that. While the personnel were not particularly concerned about the planes and the battleships, those in charge had to consider these elements to function adequately. What they found was a routine that finally was much more satisfactory than they'd hoped for. And that was this: first of all, where did the Navy boot camp personnel congregate? That was where the learning was going to take place. They congregated in, of all places, the head. And that's where they decided that the learning should take place.

What would make them learn more in the head than anywhere else? Again, studying their habit patterns, the Navy found that the men congregated in the head because it was the furthest place from view of the non-commissioned officers. The sailors could do things there which were really not permissible, such as gambling. The NCO's realized that they could introduce a form of gambling into their method, which they did.

How do you introduce gambling in a learning situation and in a constructive manner? That was the problem. The solution was to have a pinball-type machine. When you pressed a lever, you got a question. A question that was worth so many points. It had to be worth points as a basis for betting on something. And if you can bet on a higher score, then you have motivation. Now the questions were the kinds of questions that normally would bore the pants off these people but for points, and then for money, the questions took on importance, i.e., what was the safety valve number that is essential for such and such a gauge? If the valve number were higher than the given one, a machine would explode; if it were lower, the machine wouldn't run, etc. The sailor pressed the lever to start and received a multiple choice option with four choices. And then a couple of people would congregate, and one would press the lever and say "I bet I can get a higher score on this than you can." Somebody else would then come along and say, "I'll hold the money," and so on, and the result was that the fellow who was holding the money was ready, and he found out the right answer to challenge somebody else, and before long you had a whole group congregating, betting each other on who would get the highest score and every single person learning the numbers they had to know, for the various gauges, and various responses. It was almost perfect, but the problem of the transfer of training came in. They had trouble when they got on a real ship. They had to do all their work in the toilet.

The basic principle is the one that counts. If you are involved in a library orientation program you have to try to utilize some of the same aspects that we are discussing today. You can use some of these principles. For example, suppose that you were to give the usual orientation. I'm sure that you all are very, very ingenious about the things you do and maybe some of you are already doing some of the things I will mention. But obviously a straight lecture does no good, because people just don't listen. Now what can result is, of course, you confront the students when they're desperate, when they come in the library and they've got a term paper due. Then they're ready to learn. They're ready to lean on you. That's when you get the most activity. So that's very good.

But you want to take it a step further than that. Suppose that you don't want that rush towards the end of the term. You want to get them early enough. Are there things that you can do that will get them early enough? For example, a library orientation period is scheduled by having several individuals sit around together in groups of say five or so (and why do I say five? If the group is much larger than five, there's an impersonality about the session), and you give them a problem. And suppose you had four or five different groups of five, and you wanted to see who could solve a problem that involves something intriguing the quickest. Now if you are involved in term papers, you've got it. Suppose it's before the term papers are due. Are there areas of special interest to students? Are there ideas that they normally don't think of using the library for which they could use it? These are the kinds of problems that are the most fun for them.

Perhaps they have a strong interest in rock music. How do you find out the source for the top 40 songs every week? That would be the kind of topic that I would perhaps choose for a group of people. The reason I think of rock music myself is because my son went through the University of Michigan and he was in the honors program. He wrote a paper every semester for at least one of the honors courses. In the four years that he was there, every single paper had something to do with rock music. The psychology of rock music, the geography of rock music, the history of rock music, and so forth. So I know that it works. It works! In order for him not to be bored to death he found some interest and followed it through; no matter what the subject was it came out the same way. And you guessed it. He's now a rock musician.

The idea is that when functioning along this line you try to pick something that has tremendous appeal to students, something that is not directly related to what they associate as boring. The social aspect is also very important, that of having a group of four or five work together. People respond very differently in a group than they do as individuals. When they are in a group, they seek a niche within that group. And that is best utilized when there is an opportunity to talk and discuss, and they pick up from the discussion. Even the quiet ones, even the student who is very quiet, will pick up a great deal from the discussion among the others. And if the group is basically one that isn't overly dominated by someone, they will learn a great deal about the activity that is underway.

The library is an environment and I believe that environment has a tremendous influence, a tremendous influence on learning. We have not made use of the environment effectively over the past few years. We used to have much greater use of the environment than we do. I'll give you an example. When you use your bed, as many students do, as a place for studying, what happens? You go to sleep. Because the bed is the best environment for sleeping, but not for studying. You can help the students to learn that there are study rooms, and how to use a study room.

When I was a doctoral student at Michigan I was fortunate

enough to have a carrel. I used the carrel very effectively. I had a job waiting for me if I had a Ph.D. by the end of the summer session. I had taken a year to gather my materials and I had very little time, six weeks, for writing my dissertation. And I didn't know quite how to go about it. For a few days I was walking around in a state of panic. And then it occurred to me that I'm going to use my carrel effectively because that's my learning environment. And what I did was – I put on what became my writing uniform, an old dirty sweatshirt and a pair of pants and I went to my carrel and when I got in my carrel, I wrote. And as soon as I stopped writing, if I were to stop for more than two minutes, I immediately got out of that carrel, and moved away. Because I would be using my learning environment, my writing environment for some other activity, like daydreaming, worrying, fearing, all these things. And so I wouldn't do that; I got up and moved out. Then I would stay out for 20 minutes, come back in, and start to write again. In six weeks I wrote over 250 pages. Believe it or not, I didn't even have to have the paper edited. It became my final copy; my first writing was my last writing. The learning environment was so terribly important, I learned how to use it.

And I'm not above telling my own students in class that when they come to my class, I want to see them dressed for learning in the class. Not forcing it on them but attempting to teach them. If I go home for example, I immediately take off my teaching clothes. I take off my tie and take off my jacket, because I know that if I were to walk around the house with my tie and jacket on, I would start grading the meals, and then I'd really be in trouble. I would act very professorial instead of acting like a husband and a father. My point is that the environment is terribly important. And we have to teach students how to utilize that environment. And the most obvious environment for study is the library.

INSTRUCTIONAL DEVELOPMENT
IN LIBRARY USE EDUCATION

Larry Hardesty
Head, Reference Department
Roy O. West Library
DePauw University

Introduction

During the past thirty-five years a field has evolved within education known as instructional development. No doubt instructional development principles have long been practiced in one form or another, but the modern history of instructional development began during World War II with the need to train large numbers of armed forces personnel in a short period of time. Later significant contributions were made to instructional development by the theories of B. F. Skinner and the application of those theories to programmed learning.

Instructional developers now have created a series of techniques used in the instructional development process. Such techniques include the writing of behavioral objectives, learner analysis, task analysis, examining the conditions under which the learning is to occur, pilot testing, formative evaluation, and repeated revision. This list of techniques is lengthy, and these techniques undoubtedly can be useful in our efforts to develop effective bibliographic instruction programs.

Today, however, I will not be talking about these specific techniques of instructional development. Rather I am going to discuss the relationship of instructional development to bibliographic instruction from another point of view -- how the educational methods derived from the instructional development process are actually used. Recently I saw a Peanuts cartoon which emphasized the point I want to make today. It went something like this:

Charlie Brown: Sally, what did you do in school today?

Sally: I signed up for my classes. I signed up for pottery making, swimming, communication techniques, and current

> events. I got reading, writing, history, and two periods of study hall.
>
> Charlie Brown: Well, what did you learn in school today?
>
> Sally: I learned what you sign up for and what you get are two different things.

The point of this illustration is that the various instructional methods created by instructional developers using the process I outlined and the predominant instructional methods used in most schools today are two different things.

During the past thirty-five years considerable amounts of money, effort, and expertise have been directed towards the development of teaching methods such as programmed learning, computer-assisted instruction, instructional games, and educational media such as instructional television. However, the predominant teaching method in this country remains the teacher standing in the front of the self-contained classroom talking to a group of twenty to thirty students.

In the college classroom this method usually involves the students taking notes, which the professor expects the students to commit to memory. On occasion the professor may use the blackboard to explain or emphasize important points to be included in the notes. These notes are often supplemented by readings from a textbook and perhaps even some additional work in the library.

I am not suggesting that this method is necessarily ineffective. What I am suggesting is that there is little empirical evidence to support the strong belief that the lecture is the most effective method of instruction in a wide variety of situations. Ivor Davies in his book *Competency Based Learning* writes that after examining mountains of data and reviews of the literature one key point stands out: there are no significant differences in terms of learning among the teaching methods available today.(1)

The question that instructional developers are having to face today, and a question that we as librarians promoting bibliographic instruction must face, is why are not a wider variety of teaching methods, including bibliographic instruction, being used today? Library literature contains some information on this subject as it relates to bibliographic instruction; but I want to draw upon the growing body of knowledge on the communication and adoption of innovation that is coming out of such fields are rural sociology, social psychology, and education.

A key issue, I believe, in reaching the students through bibliographic instruction is getting the classroom instructors to accept student use of the library as a viable instructional method. This acceptance is important whether we are talking about course-integrated bibliographic instruction or separate courses of bibliographic instruction because the evidence shows that it is the classroom instructor who determines the amount of use the student makes of the library. However, as many of us already know, gaining the classroom instructor's acceptance of bibliographic instruction is not always easy.

Despite the popular belief that we live in an age of unprecedented change, securing the acceptance of a new idea or the adoption of an innovation often is difficult. In the commercial marketplace, it has been estimated that only *one* idea out of more than every five hundred results in a successful new product.(2) Only about eight percent of the more than 6,000 new consumer products introduced each year have a life expectancy of even one year.(3) Innovations, whether they be in business, agriculture, education, or librarianship, often have a short life, or are adopted only after many years of struggle.

Education contains many examples of the struggles involved in gaining the acceptance of an innovation. Kindergarten is just one example. After its initial introduction into the United States before the turn of the century, more than fifty years lapsed before it was widely adopted during the 1930's and 1940's. In fact, it has been estimated that public education has a fifty-year time lag. A popular prediction based on past history is that it will be approximately the year 2000 before the current movement of educational reform started after World War II will be successful.(4) Even with the education crisis created by Sputnik many school systems remain virtually untouched by the huge federal and state expenditures promoting educational reform during the past twenty years.

Ernest House, writing in his book *The Politics of Educational Innovation*, asks the question, "How can so much effort directed toward changing the school produce so little change?"(5) Another writer in this area compares educational institutions with blobs of jello in that they absorb attempts to change their shapes. New programs sometimes make dents, but soon afterwards the institution springs back to its original shape, and the influence of the innovation disappears without a trace.(6)

With all the enthusiasm generated towards bibliographic instruction during the 1970's we must remember both that it is an innovation since it is not firmly established in higher education, and at the same time it is not a new idea. Librarians have been promoting bibliographic instruction in one form or another for many years, and it is often difficult to appreciate the efforts that have gone before us. We may have even lost ground over the years.

In a recent issue of *The Journal of Academic Librarianship*, Beatrice Beech of Western Michigan University reports that in 1925 that school had a program of ten lessons in library use required for all freshmen. Today, however, she reports that they have no required program and find it difficult to convince the administration that any course in the use of the library is necessary. She asks, "I wonder if other libraries have gone through the same evolution?"(7)

The answer appears to be "yes." Kenneth Brough, in his book *Scholar's Workshop*, traces the early history of the attempt to teach students how to use the academic library. As early as the 1820's Harvard University had a library regulation stipulating that "The Librarian is to give to the Undergraduates an occasional lecture on the Library."(8) Before the College Library Section of the American Library Association in 1897, Librarian Baker of Columbia University stated:

> Almost every year since I have been connected with the Columbia University Library (since 1883) there has been something attempted toward the instruction of students in the use of the library.(9)

Peter Hernon, a doctoral student at Indiana University, has been researching the early history of library instruction. He has reported to me that up to 1913 some twenty colleges and universities required all freshmen or a similar group to take a course in library instruction. Approximately twice as many schools offered non--credit courses in library use taught by members of the library staff.(10)

Johnnie Givens, in volume IV of the *Advances in Librarianship*, traces the history of library instruction since the 1930's when there were numerous efforts to establish programs.(11) Despite the widespread efforts of that decade, in 1953 Brough still perceived the situation as bleak:

> Despite repeated insistence on the importance of teaching students how to use the library, and despite enthusiastic though sporadic attempts to reach this goal, the provision of effective instruction in bibliography and library mechanics for the great masses of university students -- especially for the freshmen -- remains an unsolved problem.(12)

Writing during the late 1960's Barbara Phipps reached a similar conclusion. In a survey she found that eighty--one percent of the 157 responding libraries reported giving some form of library instruction. However, fifty--seven percent of those responding indicated that their programs were failing to meet their needs.(13) This should give you the idea, if you do not already have it, that the adoption of bibliographic instruction is not inevitable despite our current interest and enthusiasm. One only needs to read through the report by Patricia Knapp on the Monteith College Library Experiment, one of the more carefully planned and studied attempts at bibliographic instruction, to gain a sense of the difficulties and frustrations that can arise in attempting to secure the adoption of a program of bibliographic instruction.(14)

Promoting a Program of Bibliographic Instruction

There is a body of research that may aid us in our efforts. Librarians interested in bibliographic instruction are not the only people who are infected with the missionary spirit. Studies have been conducted on topics as diverse as influencing farmers to plant new varieties of crops to convincing physicians of the merits of a new drug. The researchers' findings from such studies are highly relevant to our efforts to promote bibliographic instruction. Today I plan to present a sample of their conclusions and relate them to our efforts. Also, in an attempt to be a good librarian, I will recommend a few choice readings on the topic.

While we may talk about living in a rapidly changing world, there also is considerable resistance to change, as I have already pointed out. This resistance is natural, and it is not necessarily bad. Goodwin Watson, writing in the book *The Planning of Change*, notes that "all the forces which contribute to stability in personality or in social systems can be perceived as resisting change."(15) Without some level of resistance, there would be no stability. If we accepted every new idea or, in a more negative sense, "fad" that came along, our lives would soon become intolerable.

There are many factors that work against change, and a plan for promoting change has been shown to be an essential ingredient for a successful change effort. In an important study of major innovative projects in education conducted during the past seventy-five years, the authors conclude that: "A change initiated in a particular school, in the absence of a plan . . . is not likely to become widely or firmly entrenched."(16) There are several factors that research indicates should be considered in a plan for promoting a particular change.

A change agent, as the promoter of change is often termed, needs to consider 1) the characteristics of the innovation itself; 2) the social system in which the change is being promoted; and 3) the process through which individuals accept or reject the innovation, including useful strategies for promoting change within this process. But even before we consider these factors, we need to consider our own roles as change agents.

The Change Agent

Several writers in this field advise change agents to first examine their own motives before embarking on a campaign to modify the behavior and ideas of others. Change agents who seek to

> ... gain personal attention, dramatize differences between them--selves and others, and criticize and attack the system can be sure they will program themselves open and hostile opposition. They are their own best enemies.(17)

The successful change agent often is the one who promotes change quietly and without fanfare.(18)

Too often change agents exhibit a "true believer" syndrome, and problems can develop with high expectations and grandiose plans, which inevitably are doomed to some degree of failure. Sometimes change agents exhibit an overwhelming urgency to start a program with little or no planning. This attitude is often expressed as "Let's get started and we'll find out just what we're doing as we go along." (19) In listing the desirable characteristics of change agents, researchers usually include such characteristics as patience, willingness to work hard, and courage. These are needed to help overcome fantasies and stereotypes so confidence can be built, which is necessary for help to be offered and accepted.(20)

Researchers have noted that change agents must be careful in committing their time and energy. Numerous innovations are dropped when the promoters "burn out." Too often change efforts begin with a vengeance and last only a year or so because the individuals involved cannot maintain the pace to which they have committed themselves.(21) A delicate balance needs to be maintained between enough enthusiasm to maintain the change effort in the face of resistance and not so much enthusiasm that careful planning is overlooked.

The Innovation

The characteristics of an innovation are important, but what is significant is not how the change agent views the innovation, but how the potential adopter views the innovation. In fact, the actual characteristics of an innovation may have little impact on the adoption of the innovation. Matthew Miles includes in his book *Innovation in Education* that:

> Educational innovations are almost never installed on their own merits. Characteristics of the local system, of the innovating person or group, and of other relevant groups, often outweigh the impact of what the innovation is.(22)

Seldom is the fact that a change might be a good idea sufficient for the change to be accepted. This in itself is a discouraging idea for those of us, like myself, who sometimes think that bibliographic instruction is such a good idea that its adoption is inevitable.

Research indicates that the view classroom instructors have of bibliographic instruction is critical. Richard Evans, in his classical study on the acceptance of instructional television, *Resistance to Innovation in Higher Education*, concludes that students would be less hostile toward instructional television if their attitudes were not influenced considerably by those of their teachers.(23) In the library profession, Patricia Knapp found that students' "need" to use the academic library is usually derived from the value placed upon such work by their instructors.(24)

In *The Planning of Change*, Goodwin Watson observes that resistance to change can be reduced if change agents are able to empathize with potential adopters, to recognize valid objections, and to take steps to relieve unnecessary fears.(25) As librarians, for example, we need to anticipate and appreciate how classroom instructors view bibliographic instruction. Recently, I attended a conference at Earlham College and listened to a classroom instructor speak very forcefully about the importance of bibliographic instruction in his classes. However, he ended his talk with a brief plea for librarians to understand that bibliographic instruction might not be appropriate for the goals of every class. Perhaps he had a point, and we need to step into the shoes of classroom instructors more often and view the characteristics of bibliographic instruction.

Everett Rogers has written what I think is the best book available on the topic of promoting the adoption of new ideas. Its title is *Communication of Innovation*. In this book he reports his conclusions after examining literally hundreds of studies on the adoption of new ideas. Some of his conclusions deal with the characteristics of innovations that affect their adoption; perhaps we can relate them to our efforts to promote the adoption of bibliographic instruction. We must keep in mind that these characteristics are especially important with respect to how classroom instructors view them, rather than our own attitudes.

Rogers lists relative advantage as the first characteristic of an innovation he considers important. Relative advantage he defines as:

> The degree to which an innovation is perceived by the adopter as

better than the idea it supersedes. The greater the perceived relative advantage of an innovation, the more rapid its rate of adoption.(26)

Classroom faculty and students may view bibliographic instruction in a different light than librarians. Patricia Knapp concludes from her experience that:

> Most college faculty members see library instruction as dealing with bits of information, undeniably useful, but fragmented, not related to any single, coherent framework, not calling for problem-solving behavior, for critical thinking, for imagination. Most college students see it as sheer high school busy work.(27)

Relative advantage includes considerations such as will the innovation increase the teaching load, increase the time needed to grade papers, or decrease the time needed for class preparation and research.

A second important characteristic of an innovation discussed by Rogers is compatibility. Compatibility is:

> The degree to which an innovation is perceived by the adopter as being consistent with existing values, past experiences, and the needs of the receivers.(28)

Matthew Miles points out, "An innovation regarded as a means of reducing a well-known gap between ideals and practice may achieve adoption."(29)

There appears to be potential usefulness of this approach in bibliographic instruction. In an article in *College & Research Libraries* titled "College Libraries -- Indicated Failures: Some Reasons -- and a Possible Remedy," Robert Blackburn notes that:

> Everybody says the library is the heart of the college. Everybody is for the library . . . . Why is there an unsuccessful marriage based on love between students and books when both faculty and librarians claim this as their end and when all conditions seem to make the goal inevitable?(30)

The answer he provides is that there are several points of conflict between librarians and classroom instructors.

One area of conflict concerns the control of students and the control of books. Blackburn hypothesizes that faculty members want to control books even more than they want students to love the books, and who appears to control the books? The librarians.(31)

The classroom teacher may be very well aware how useful books are in educating the student. In fact, books may be viewed by some instructors as a source of competition since ideas contrary to the instructor's or unknown to the instructor may be expressed in the library's books.(32)

On the other hand, librarians may resent the classroom instructors' control over what the students read due to assignments. Blackburn also observes that classroom instructors may regulate to a large degree what books and what journals the library may have.(33)

Classroom instructors often do not view librarians as peers, and this is a problem in promoting bibliographic instruction. Ronald Havelock in his research on the promoting of change concludes that individuals tend to compare themselves to persons with similar backgrounds and similar status levels.(34) Patricia Knapp's experience supported this conclusion.(35) In my own experience I have often found one classroom instructor can be more effective in selling another classroom instructor on the merits of bibliographic instruction than I can.

We often face problems in promoting bibliographic instruction because of the different emphasis classroom faculty place on the library and their lack of previous experience with librarians as classroom teachers. In a survey of the humanities and social science faculty at DePauw University I received the following responses to this statement:

Optimum use of a college library as a learning tool depends upon the following conditions. Please rank in order of importance. [The following indicates first place ranking.]

36 (55%)   The maintenance of collections which are adequate in size and scope to support independent study and investigation.

21 (32%)   Faculty presentations of a kind which inspire students to use the resources of the library intensively.

8 (12%)   Library instruction which will enable students to use the library effectively.

I suspect that a group of librarians might rank these statements in a different order. This ranking probably reflects what Evan Farber refers to as the "university–library syndrome" of classroom instructors. This syndrome is the strong emphasis on large library collections that classroom faculty often have as a result of their graduate school training at the large research institutions most of them attended.(36)

A second question I asked in the survey was:

In your graduate work, how did you learn to use the library resources? (Please circle *all* appropriate items.)

58 (88%) a. Learned through My Own Efforts

31 (47%) b. Learned from Other Graduate Students

34 (52%) c. Learned through Informal Consultation with Professors

21 (32%) d. Learned in a Graduate Course in (or as Part of a Course in) Library Usage Taught by a Departmental Instructor

34 (52%) e. Learned through Informal Consultation with a Librarian

5 (8%) f. Learned in a Graduate Course in Library Usage Taught by a Librarian

1 g. No Need for Use of Library Resources in My Graduate Work

Such responses indicate that at least at DePauw University many of the classroom instructors have had little contact with librarians as formal instructors in library use.

Bibliographic instruction may not be compatible with other values and experiences held by instructors. Bibliographic instruction tends to be process oriented while many classroom instructors tend to emphasize the accumulation of knowledge. This has been characterized as being student--centered as opposed to being discipline--centered.

From instructional development several patterns have emerged in terms of teacher acceptance of methods of instruction. One is that instructors tend to resist instructional methods which result in them having less control over the classroom and the student. Instructors also tend to resist change that may lessen their position as authorities in the subject, or that will place them in a vulnerable position of having to learn about another's field.(37) Perhaps it is no wonder that Patricia Knapp found that often classroom teachers believed that all instruction about bibliographic work should be done by them,(38) or that it was the province of the classroom teacher -- not librarians -- to recommend sources of information.(39)

Another evident pattern is that frequently teachers will not fully accept certain methods of instruction because of their definitions of teaching. Researchers find that instructors often define teaching as capturing and holding the attention of a number of students, and serving as the continuous mediator between students and information. Evans states that instructional television was resisted because instructors viewed it as lacking the ingredients of personal contact between teacher and students, feedback from students, and proper supervision of students.(40)

There appears to be a natural law of program survival. Instructors have a tendency to emphasize those elements of an instructional method that are most compatible with their experiences and values and to de-emphasize the elements that are not.(41) In a major study on programmed learning, Richard Carlson, in *Adoptions of Educational Innovations*, reports that a group of teachers viewed programmed learning as a threat to their concept of teaching and consciously or unconsciously did several things to counter its effectiveness.(42) The programmed instruction was designed to let students work at their own rate, but the teachers involved in the study prevented this. Through various methods they restricted the faster students and allowed the slower students to keep pace. In the end, the programmed instruction method began to look very similar to the regular classroom instruction methods used previously.(43)

A third characteristic discussed by Rogers is complexity. Complexity is:

> The degree to which an innovation is perceived as difficult to understand and use.(44)

Evans points out that the high rate of failure of audio-visual programs might well be traced to the amount of hardware and effort required on the part of schools and instructors to use the equipment.(45) Other researchers note that the success or failure of several of the major curriculum reform efforts during the 1960's could be attributed to the degree of complexity. The American physics curriculum reform of that decade had a slow rate of adoption because it had a materials-centered approach, but the developers had no deliberate plan of providing materials to the teachers. On the other hand, the science and mathematics programs developed by the National Science Foundation were widely adopted because they were designed as complete units for use by individual teachers.(46)

We must consider how well classroom instructors understand what we mean by bibliographic instruction. Are we requiring them to learn new skills, and how much effort is involved for them to continue bibliographic instruction? Considering the general experiences librarians seem to have with classroom faculty using the library and assigned library work, it seems to me that bibliographic instruction probably does appear complex to many classroom instructors. With reference to complexity, some researchers note that resistance to an innovation based on a lack of understanding may be lessened if the participants, in this case the classroom instructors, can be brought into the diagnostic efforts leading them to agree on what the basic problems are and their importance.(47)

Trialability or divisibility is the fourth characteristic of an innovation that Rogers lists. It is:

> . . . the degree to which an innovation may be experimented with on a limited basis.(48)

Innovations requiring large expenditures of time, money, or effort by the adopting person or group are likely to move slowly.(49) I like the advice Jim Kennedy of Earlham College gave at this conference a few years ago. Jim suggested that librarians should be like the Volkswagen people and "think small" – in the beginning anyway.(50) Innovations that meet this condition are those that can be tried on a small scale, on a partial basis, and for a short period of time. This also refers to the number of individuals or proportion of the group who need to be involved.(51) It appears that bibliographic instruction is quite trialable.

A final characteristic listed by Rogers is observability or communicability. This is:

> . . . the degree to which the results of an innovation are visible to others.(52)

An important question to consider is how easy or how difficult it is to explain or demonstrate the worth of an innovation. Again we are dealing with perceived worth rather than what might be the actual worth. Instructors may see a method as being less effective when research might show no significant differences.

In promoting the reform of the physics curriculum during the 1960's, researchers found that the new syllabus was not widely adopted where demonstrations and courses were held in special institutes. However, the syllabus was widely adopted when such demonstrations and courses were held in model classrooms where teachers in the local area could view the programs in action.(53) I have found it quite effective to communicate the worth of bibliographic instruction by simply taking selected members of the DePauw University classroom instructors to Earlham College to talk with the librarians, classroom instructors, and students. Unfortunately not everyone can work at a college a short drive from Earlham. Also, a key question is how effectively the visitors can convey to their colleagues back at DePauw University the value of the Earlham College library instruction program.

The Social System

Characteristics of the social system or structure are a second major consideration in the promotion of an innovation. Again it is Patricia Knapp in the library profession who has given the most attention to the relationship between the social structure of the academic community and bibliographic instruction.(54) Evan Farber of Earlham College also has pointed out the importance of the "closely knit sense of community and very informal relationships among students, faculty, administration, and staff" at the institution in providing favorable conditions for bibliography instruction.(55)

The institution may encourage or discourage innovations. Encouragement or discouragement may come through the formal reward structure such as the criteria used for tenure, promotion, and salary increases. Another method may be the way the institution allows teachers to interact with one another. Methods such as team teaching allow instructors to view each other and may result in them rewarding and supporting mutual efforts to improve their teaching by trying innovative methods. This may occur completely outside the formal reward structure of the institution.

In general, researchers emphasize the role of a limited number of individuals in the social system. In attempting any planned change, "legitimacy for the change must be gained through obtaining the support of key people."(56) These people are not necessarily the formal leaders of the organization.(57) They may be those deemed the "opinion leaders" because of the way they are able to influence informally the attitudes and actions of others.(58) Perhaps the best clue for identifying opinion leaders is the extent to which other people seek them out for advice or listen attentively when they speak.(59) Rogers concludes that the success of a change agent is positively related to the extent that he or she works through these opinion leaders.(60) Patricia Knapp notes their importance in the Monteith College Project when she observes that "the support of a powerful member of the staff could practically guarantee an initial hearing for our ideas."(61)

Generally all members of a social system do not adopt a new idea at the same time. Instead, according to Rogers, they adopt in "an ordered time sequence,"(62) and may be grouped in adopter categories. He finds that adopter distributions follow a bell-shaped curve over time.(63) On the basis of their relative disposition toward innovation, members of a social system can be divided into the following five categories:

      Innovators
      Early Adopters
      Early Majority
      Late Majority
      Resisters

Innovators are venturesome. They are the first persons in the social system to adopt an innovation. They tend to be intelligent, eager to try new ideas, and willing to take risks. They are generally the individuals most receptive to change. However, innovators tend to be individualists and usually not integrated into the prevailing social structure.(64) Seldom are they opinion leaders in the social system. There are good reasons for a change agent not to work with innovators. First, they are usually too innovative to serve as models for the rest of the members of the social system. Second, innovators are often quick to drop new ideas.

The next category is the early adopters. This group may contain opinion leaders, depending on the social system. In fact, this adopter category, more than any other, usually has the greatest degree of opinion leadership in most social systems.(65) They tend to be respected, knowledgeable members of the social system. The early adopter is often considered the "person to check with" before using a new idea.(66)

The members of the early majority group are deliberate. They tend to adopt new ideas just before the average member of a social system. This group tends to be followers instead of leaders.(67)

The late majority group are the skeptics. They adopt new ideas just after the average member of the social system. They can be persuaded, but the weight of the norms of the social system must definitely favor the innovation before the late majority are convinced.(68)

The resisters are the last to adopt an innovation. Generally they are not opinion leaders and may be almost completely isolated within the social system. By the time they adopt an innovation, it may already have been superseded by a more recent idea which the first group is already using.(69) Such persons can sometimes destroy an innovative program, and the change agent must try to identify them and invest extra effort to influence them or at least neutralize them. Members of this group often stand on tradition or the status quo.

It is important that a change agent be able to identify individuals in the social system in terms of their innovative group so the change agent can know where and how to concentrate his or her energies and time. Identification of and work with opinion leaders is crucial, but one must also identify the other members of the social system in terms of these broad groups. A change agent should be aware of the formal and informal groupings in the social system. Informal groupings, such as lunch groups, are particularly important since the individuals come together voluntarily and often influence each other to a high degree. A late majority person may be influenced in a desired direction if a change agent is able to convince an opinion leader of the same informal group to adopt an innovation.

The Individual

Researchers have concluded that an individual's decision about an innovation is not an instantaneous act. Rather it is a process that occurs over a period of time and consists of a series of actions. One model of the process, as described by Rogers, is the social interaction model.

The social interaction model theorizes that individuals go through five stages in considering the adoption of a new idea. The first stage is the awareness stage. It is at this stage that the individual first learns of the existence of an innovation, but lacks complete information about it.(70) Generally this awareness of the existence of an innovation comes not as the result of a need; rather the awareness creates the need.(71) This happens all the time through the mass media. We are constantly discovering the need for gadgets and devices that we never knew we needed.

The second stage is the interest stage. At this stage the individual develops an interest in the innovation and seeks additional information about it.(72) This stage consists of information gathering activities and implies some degree of personal commitment.

The third stage is the evaluation stage. The individual makes mental application of the innovation to his or her situation and decides whether or not to try it.(73) The individual may move quickly into the next stage, which is the trial stage. Here the individual applies the innovation on a small scale to determine its utility. (74) Finally, the individual may reach the adoption stage. The individual considers the results of the evaluation and trial stages and decides whether to adopt or reject the innovation.(75) It must be remembered that the trial stage may be quite extended. Once the innovation is adopted, then the individual uses it continuously on a full scale.

A second model is the problem--solving model which emphasizes the role of the adopter of an innovation in solving a perceived problem. A change agent may initiate the change process, but the emphasis is on the potential adopter desiring the change and fully participating in the process of creating the change. Change agents using this model focus on the potential adopter as the starting place and the role of diagnosis in the identification of possible solutions. The change agent role is non--directive in that he or she does not take over the problem--solving of the adopter, but does provide guidance. Local resources and expertise are considered important in solving the problem or filling the need. The supposed advantage of this model is that the adopter will not only accept the innovation, but will also internalize it since the change is viewed as a free choice in response to a specific need.(76)

From an instructional development point of view there are some difficulties in applying this model to bibliographic instruction. In the first place, we are limiting ourselves to one method, however useful, in solving an instructional problem (that being bibliographic instruction). However, if that is understood from the beginning, then the problem--solving model may be quite useful. It appears to be less manipulative, in a negative sense, than other techniques, and I am attempting to apply it to some elements of the CLR--NEH grant program I am directing at DePauw University.

Briefly, I am providing small grants to individuals or groups of classroom instructors as compensation for writing general goals statements concerning the skills graduating students should have in particular disciplines. The next step is to determine if the students have those skills, and then if they do not, how to insure that the students develop the skills. At each stage the classroom instructors participate in the problem--solving. Right now it is too early to determine the success of this element of the grant program, but early results are encouraging.

Strategies

Research indicates that certain adoption strategies work at different stages of the adoption process. Egon Guba, a professor of education at Indiana University, has suggested six general categories of adoption strategies: telling, showing, helping, involving, training, and intervening.(77) They relate more closely to the social interaction model, but also incorporate elements of the problem--solving model.

Telling is communication with written or spoken words. This might take the form of newsletters, brochures, speeches, informal conversations, and mass media communications. Evidence suggests that the media tends to play an important role at the awareness and interest stage, but tactics such as using printed materials do little to convince people to try or adopt an innovation. Ivor Morrish in his book *Aspects of Educational Change* reports that in certain sociological studies media and commercial sources were the first to bring news of an innovation; but friends, colleagues, and professional sources were required to legitimate decisions to adopt or reject the innovation.(78)

Showing is communication that involves direct contact with an innovation through observation. This can include demonstrations, slides, and classroom visits. Getting instructors to visit the classroom of another instructor where bibliographic instruction is being pre--sented may be a useful technique. I have used this technique -- but with care -- since the instructors first must have a certain amount of trust and respect for each other.

Helping is direct involvement of the change agent in the affairs of the client, *on the client's terms*. This may take the form of con--sultation or trouble shooting. Probably the potential adopter must have reached the trial stage before this strategy is attempted. This technique is emphasized in the problem--solving model. It must be used carefully since it is easy to move from helping to intervening, and the instructor may resent what can be perceived as an intrusion of the librarian into his or her classroom.

Involving requires participation of the potential adopter. This strategy may include asking an instructor to help solve a particular teaching problem, to talk about how his or her students use the library, or to discuss students' ability to use the library. Sometimes an instructor who is using bibliographic instruction on a trial basis might be asked to explain the methods to another instructor; through this the instructor may become even more committed to the use of bibliographic instruction.

Training consists of familiarizing potential adopters with a proposed new idea. It may involve assisting them to increase their skills or alter their attitudes. Workshops and in--service training may be offered, and this strategy can include other strategies, such as telling, showing, helping, and involving. Sometimes the instructor being present in the classroom when the students are being given bibliographic instruction results in a certain amount of training.

Intervening is a strategy in which the change agent is directly involved on his or her own terms, rather than the potential adopter's terms. It seldom happens in bibliographic instruction since in general librarians lack the clout to use it successfully. It involves mandating certain actions, such as forcing the adoption of certain textbooks. It is a high risk strategy since the backlash can seriously threaten the success of an innovation.

Various techniques with these strategies work with different effectiveness. Bringing in an outside expert to lecture on an innova--tion often is ineffective, particularly if careful preparation does not precede the visit. A visit to another school that has adopted an innovation is supposed to be very effective, and I think my experience with Earlham College has confirmed this.

There is one technique which research indicates works at all stages of the adoption process. It is personal contact. Ernest House in his book *Politics of Educational Innovation* emphasizes his conclusion that most innovations are dependent on face-to-face personal contacts. He believes that personal contacts determine the frequency and occurrence of innovations, and it is through this medium that most innovations are adopted.(79)

This method may be of particular importance to librarians. There are few serious studies of librarian-classroom instructor relationships, but an article in the March 1975 issue of the *Pennsylvania Library Association Bulletin* presents the results of such a study by a librarian and a psychologist. It is titled "Face the Faculty: Prevalent Attitudes Regarding Librarianship Faculty Relationships." The authors conclude that: "Poor communications is the prime area of difficulty between librarians and faculty."(80) Often classroom faculty are unaware of library problems and procedures and librarians often are unaware of curriculum developments and needs. Many libraries, observe these researchers, apparently lack formal methods of informing the classroom faculty of the services of the library.(81)

Conclusion

In conclusion, I think that the models and strategies developed from the experience of instructional developers and others do have considerable application to our efforts to promote bibliographic instruction. We do live in a time of change. There is no shortage of innovations or fads, as some might be called, which can demand the time and energy of both librarians and classroom instructors. However, planned change is a slow process and success is very elusive.

We need to be realistic in establishing our goals and in examining our motives for seeking these goals. We need to be careful in creating new programs that might require large amounts of time and energy at levels which we may not be able to sustain over a long period of time. We need to develop a group of supporters both within the library staff and within the ranks of the classroom instructors to share our efforts. Mechanisms of feedback must be incorporated into our programs so we can have the information needed for continual improvement. Finally, if bibliographic instruction is to become institutionalized, continual reinforcement for both our efforts and the efforts of the classroom instructors must be an important part of bibliographic instruction.

If I have convinced you of the difficulty of promoting bibliographic instruction and the need for careful planning, I have accomplished my purpose. However, I trust I have not convinced you of the impossibility of success. Changes do occur and they can be planned and predicted. I hope I have made you aware of some of the factors that need to be considered and some of the methods that may be useful.

Willingness to work hard and enthusiasm, however desirable and necessary these qualities are, are not alone sufficient to insure the successful adoption of a new idea. Careful planning and promotion of a program are crucial elements if bibliographic instruction is to become a permanent part of higher education. I thank you for this opportunity to speak before you, and welcome the opportunity to talk with many of you individually and exchange ideas over the next two days. I also would be glad to answer any questions you may have now.

FOOTNOTES

1. Ivor Davies, *Competency Based Learning* (New York: Mc Graw--Hill Book Company, 1973) p161.

2. Elizabeth Martin, *New Products, New Profits* (New York: American Management Association, 1964) p9, as cited by Everett M. Rogers, *Communication of Innovation* (New York: The Free Press, 1971) p68.

3. John T. Conner, "Progress Reshapes Competition," *Printers' Ink*, Vol. 287 (1964) p36, as cited by Rogers, *Communication of Innovation*, p68.

4. Don Glines, "Why Innovative Schools Don't Remain Innovative," *The Education Digest*, Vol. XXXVIII, No. 9 (May, 1973) p5.

5. Ernest House, *The Politics of Educational Innovation* (Berkeley, California: McCutchan Publishing Corporation, 1974) p2.

6. Bill Romey, "Radical Innovation in a Conventional Framework: Problems and Prospects," *Journal of Higher Education*, Vol. XLVIII, No. 6 (November/December, 1977) p695.

7. Beatrice Beech, "The History of Library Instruction," *The Journal of Academic Librarianship*, Vol. 3, No. 4 (September, 1977) p214.

8. K.D. Metcalf, "The Undergraduate and the Harvard Library, 1765--1877," *Harvard Library Bulletin*, I (Winter, 1947) p49, as cited by Kenneth Brough, *Scholar's Workshop: Evolving Conceptions of Library Service* (Urbana, Illinois: University of Illinois Press, 1953) p152.

9. American Library Association, College Library Section (Proceedings, June 23 and 25, 1897) *Library Journal*, XXII (October, 1897), C168, as cited by Brough, *Scholar's Workshop*, p155.

10. Statement by Peter Hernon, personal interview, April 1, 1978.

11. Johnnie Givens, "The Use of Resources in the Learning Experience," *Advances in Librarianship*, ed. Melvin Voigt, Vol. 4 (New York: Academic Press, 1974) pp149--174.

12. Brough, *Scholar's Workshop*, p157.

13. Barbara Phipps, "Library Instruction for the Undergraduate," *College & Research Libraries*, Vol. 29, No. 5 (September, 1968) pp441--423.

14. Patricia B. Knapp, *The Monteith College Library Experiment* (New York: Scarecrow Press, 1966).

15. Goodwin Watson, "Resistance to Change," *The Planning of Change*, ed. Warren G. Bennis, Kenneth D. Benne, and Robert Chin (New York: Holt, Rinehart and Winston, Inc., 1969) p488.

16. Don Orlosky and B. Othanel Smith, "Educational Change: Its Origins and Characteristics," *Phi Delta Kappan*, LIII (March, 1972) p414.

17. Larry L. Palmatier, "How Teachers Can Innovate and Still Keep Their Jobs," *Journal of Teacher Education*, Vol. XXVI, No. 1 (Spring, 1975) p60.

18. *Ibid.*

19. William J. Kritek, "Lessons from the Literature on Implementation," *Educational Administration Quarterly*, Vol. 12, No. 3 (Fall, 1976) p90.

20. Richard I. Evans, *Resistance to Innovation in Higher Education* (San Francisco: Jossey--Bass, Inc. Publishers, 1968) p23.

21. Kirtek, "Lessons from the Literature," p92.

22. Matthew B. Miles, "Innovation in Education: Some Generalizations," *Innovations in Education*, ed. Matthew B. Miles (New York: Bureau of Publications, Teachers College, Columbia University, 1964) p635.

23. Evans, *Resistance to Innovation*, p69.

24. Knapp, *Monteith College*, p183.

25. Watson, "Resistance to Change," p497.

26. Everett M. Rogers, *Communication of Innovation* (New York: The Free Press, 1971) pp22--23.

27. Knapp, *Monteith College*, p183.

28. Rogers, *Communication of Innovation*, pp22–23.

29. Miles, "Innovation in Education," p638.

30. Robert T. Blackburn, "College Libraries – Indicated Failures: Some Reasons – and a Possible Remedy," *College & Research Libraries*, Vol. 29, No. 3 (May, 1968) pp171--172.

31. Blackburn, "College Libraries," p172.

32. Maurice P. Marchant, "Faculty--Librarian Conflict," *Library Journal*, Vol. 94, No. 15 (September 1, 1969) p2887.

33. Blackburn, "College Libraries," p173.

34. Ronald Havelock, *Planning for Innovation through Dissem--ination and Utilization of Knowledge* (Ann Arbor: CRUSE, Institute for Social Research, University of Michigan, 1969) pp5–13.

35. Knapp, *Monteith College*, p26.

36. Evan Farber, "Limiting College Library Growth: Bane or Boom," *The Journal of Academic Librarianship*, Vol. 1, No. 5 (November, 1975) p13.

37. Ivor Morrish, *Aspects of Educational Change* (New York: John Wiley & Sons, 1976) p87.

38. Knapp, *Monteith College*, p183.

39. *Ibid.*, p171.

40. Evans, *Resistance to Innovation*, p17.

41. Kritek, "Lessons from the Literature," p94.

42. Richard O. Carlson, *Adoption of Educational Innovations* (Eugene, Oregon: The Center for the Advanced Study of Educational Administration, 1965) p83.

43. *Ibid.*

44. Rogers, *Communication of Innovation*, p23.

45. Evans, *Resistance to Innovation*, p141.

46. Morrish, *Educational Change*, p120.

47. Watson, "Innovation in Education," p497.

48. Rogers, *Communication of Innovation*, p23.

49. Miles, "Innovation in Education," p635.

50. James Kennedy, "A Separate Course in Bibliographic Instruction," *Library Orientation*, ed. Sul Lee (Ann Arbor, 1972) p23.

51. Morrish, *Educational Change*, p76.

52. Rogers, *Communication of Innovation*, p23.

53. Morrish, *Educational Change*, p77.

54. Knapp, *Montieth College*, pp19--38.

55. Evan Farber, "Library Instruction throughout the Curriculum: Earlham College Program," *Educating the Library User*, ed. John Lubans (New York: R.R. Bowker Company, 1974) p145.

56. Warren G. Bennis and Edgar Schein, *The Planning of Change*, 2d ed. (New York: Holt, Rinehart and Winston, 1969) p354.

57. Kenneth G. Benne and Max Birnbaum, "Principles of Change," *The Planning of Change*, p333.

58. Rogers, *Communication of Innovation*, p35.

59. Alice R. Jwaideh, "Implementation Workshop: Participants Manual," (Bloomington, Indiana: UCIDT, n.d.) p14. (Mim--eographed.)

60. Rogers, *Communication of Innovation*, p233.

61. Knapp, *Monteith College*, p133.

62. Rogers, *Communication of Innovation*, p175.

63. *Ibid.*, p179.

64. Jwaideh, "Implementation," p17.

65. Rogers, *Communication of Innovation*, p184.

66. *Ibid.*

67. Jwaideh, "Implementation," p18.

68. Rogers, *Communication of Innovation*, p184.

69. *Ibid.*, p185.

70. *Ibid.*, pp100–101.

71. Morrish, *Educational Change*, p123.

72. Rogers, *Communication of Innovation*, pp100–101.

73. *Ibid.*

74. *Ibid.*

75. *Ibid.*

76. Morrish, *Educational Change*, 128.

77. Egon Guba (no citation), quoted in Jwaideh, "Implementation," p38.

78. Morrish, *Educational Change*, p125.

79. House, *Politics of Educational Change*, p3.

80. Samuel H. Cameron and Karlyn W. Messinger, "Face the Faculty: Attitudes Regarding Librarian–Faculty Relationships," *PLA Bulletin*, Vol. 30, No. 2 (March, 1975) p26.

81. *Ibid.*

TEACHING THE LIBRARIAN TO TEACH: THE SITUATION IN BRITAIN

Peter Fox
Assistant Under–Librarian
Cambridge University Library

In this talk I should like to give you a general view of the situation which confronts the British user education librarian wanting to learn how to teach, and then I want to discuss in some detail a project at the University of Surrey which is attempting to deal with this situation.

For the most part, librarians involved in user education stand up in front of a class of students or put together a course of bibliographic instruction without having received any training specifically in this aspect of their work. It is believed that many of them are aware of a need for some form of training in teaching and learning methods. This belief is confirmed by a report submitted to the British Library by the Review Committee on Education for Information Use. The report states that:

> Many librarians now engaged in teaching use of library resources have themselves had no formal training in teaching or learning methods. They are, on the whole, conscious of this deficiency, but there are at present no courses designed for teaching librarians to teach.(1)

Library School Courses

It appears that the library schools are not able to include this sort of training in their courses. As Nancy Hammond reported at this conference last year, the average postgraduate diploma or master's degree course has about 200 lecture hours to devote to the whole field of librarianship, and so it is barely feasible to include in this a course on library instruction itself, let alone the teaching of library instruction.(2) The best that can be done is to promote the ability of librarians to communicate effectively. In May 1977 the Postgraduate School of Librarianship and Information Science at the University of Sheffield held a forum for representatives of the library schools.(3) There was general agreement at this meeting that librarianship courses should be structured in such a way as to improve the students' communication skills. It was suggested that not only should much of the teaching be done through seminars and tutorials, a form of instruction in which the student plays a more active part than in a lecture, but also that simulation and role-playing exercises should be built into the course.

But even if these suggestions are carried out, they can do little more than attempt to make the librarian a better communicator. It is clear that detailed instruction on how to teach, and practice in the teaching itself, cannot be given at library schools. And perhaps the library school is the wrong place anyway; the proportion of librarians involved in teaching must be fairly small, and the number who know already at library school that they will be involved in teaching must be smaller still.

Courses for University Lecturers

So the normal library school courses are not of much specific help in teaching the librarian to teach. But the academic librarian wanting to learn this skill is in a very similar position to the young university lecturer in his first teaching post. What training does *he* get? Until a few years ago the answer would have been "precious little!" Indeed in some universities even today the only formal help a new faculty member is likely to receive is sherry with the vice-chancellor and perhaps a free copy of a book on lecturing technique. University teachers are still described as the last bastion of English amateurism. We have all heard stories of the lecturer who delivers entire lectures with his back to the students or the one who looked up from his notes at the end of the hour and found that the room was empty. It was assumed for years that the process of having spent three years writing a Ph.D. thesis meant that, by some process of osmosis, the lecturer became equipped to perform effectively in the lecture theatre or seminar room.

Many universities have recognized the fallacy of this attitude and have introduced courses in teaching methods for their new staff. These courses range in scale from the one-day "introduction to the university," which may include general advice on lecturing, to the very intensive, week-long courses run by universities such as London and Surrey. Short courses run by the University Teaching Methods Unit at the University of London, for example, have covered topics such as "Improving Your Lecturing," "Evaluation of Teaching," "Small Groups Workshop," "Applications of Programmed Learning Techniques in Education."(4) The course run jointly by the Universities of Kent and Surrey has been attended by a handful of librarians. It is usually held just before the beginning of the fall term and is open not only to participants from the host universities but to university teachers from the rest of Britain and abroad. The course aims to acquaint participants with a range of teaching techniques, not only covering the basic skills of lecturing and group teaching but also including the use of audio-visual media and other teaching aids. The items on small-group teaching, for example, are likely to be particularly valuable to librarians, as this is probably the most common method of giving library instruction. The sessions teach how to handle a group, run a discussion, tactfully subdue dominant members and encourage the withdrawn. An important feature of the course is the emphasis on the variety of teaching methods available and the fact that the teacher has to develop the ability to assess the needs of the students so that he can use the appropriate teaching methods to convey what he wants to teach.

Theoretically, because librarians in most British universities now have the same status as teaching faculty members, there is no reason why librarians who want to attend these courses should not do so. I say theoretically, because, as far as I have been able to discover, few librarians have actually been on such a course. As with most aspects of librarianship, what one needs is something which is essentially practical, where the participant can acquire some experience of teaching in front of an audience or of actually making an audio tape or tape/slide. I suspect, therefore, that many of the general one-day courses would not be appropriate, as there is simply not time to cover these practical aspects adequately. And the trouble with the longer courses is that, inevitably, they are expensive. The Surrey course which I have already mentioned, for example, costs £ 100 -- $200. Many chief librarians would be loath to spend that amount of money on sending their staff on a course which they may well regard as being peripheral to their work. That is, of course, if the librarians can even spare the time to be absent for a week in September, which is often the busiest time of the year in an academic library.

I have tried to suggest one or two reasons why the courses on teaching methods which are available are generally not attended by librarians. Perhaps it is simply that the initiative has not come from the librarians themselves, perhaps they think that they might feel out of place in such a course or that they might not benefit from a course designed for their academic colleagues.

Short Courses

Courses for user education librarians do exist. They are often run by the library schools or by the Library Association in conjunction with one or more library schools. They tend to be of two types. There is the general course on educating the user, which will include topics such as computerized information retrieval, instruction in specific subjects and evaluation of courses. If teaching methods are included at all in such a course they are usually only incidental to some other topic. The second type of course is the more specific one, concerned with teaching methods, but usually in the context of audio-visual media. Recent examples of such courses are the one held in September 1977 at the School of Librarianship, Leeds Polytechnic, called "Use of A/V in Reader Education" and two to be held in July and September 1978 at the College of Librarianship Wales, the first on the "Use and Production of AV Aids in Education and Training" and the second on "Closed Circuit TV and Video Cassettes." There are three journals which regularly provide information about such courses. The *Library Association Record* publishes a supplement called "Directory of Short Courses in Librarianship and Information Work." This appears three times a year, with the April, August and December issues of the journal. The second journal is *Infuse*, the newsletter produced by the British Library's Information Officer for User Education.(5) The third is *ISG News*, the newsletter of the Information Services Group of SCONUL (the Standing Conference of National and University Libraries).(6)

I feel that so far I have presented rather a negative picture of the situation: librarians feel that they need help with teaching methods, they do not attend the courses arranged for university teachers, and there are no courses specifically for librarians. From now on I am going to try and be more positive, and talk in particular about two projects. The first, which is still under way, is concerned with teaching and learning methods for librarians. The second is concerned not with librarians at all, but with training the university teacher to teach. The results, however, are in many ways as relevant to user education as they are to our academic colleagues.

The first project, which is funded by the British Library, is based at the University of Surrey, and is entitled "Development of a Package on Teaching and Learning Methods for Librarians." The idea of a teaching package evolved out of an earlier British Library project which set out to determine the needs of librarians in relation to teaching and learning methods. The final report of this earlier project is due to be published as a British Library Research and Development Report later this year.(4) For my information about it I am indebted to Dr. P.J. Hills of the University of Surrey, the project director. The aims of the project were threefold:

1. to consider the need to acquaint librarians with a range of teaching and learning methods and methods by which this might be carried out;

2. to consider the ways in which librarians might apply such methods to the provision of instructional material for library users;

3. to consider ways in which the whole area of possible library use by students might become a recognized part of normal course work.

A questionnaire was sent out to user education librarians to find out what teaching methods were in current use and what methods the librarians felt that they wanted to know more about. The results showed that most librarians rely heavily on the traditional lecture or seminar methods in their teaching. But many of them showed interest in learning more about audio--visual methods and practical exercises. Probably because it is one of the cheaper and simpler audio-visual media, the tape/slide presentation was mentioned particularly.

Based on the results of the questionnaire, the working party involved with the project felt that there should be a development of methods of acquainting librarians with the variety of teaching and learning methods which now exists. They listed the following as important features which such courses should cover:

Face to face methods:
    lectures
    group methods
    individual one teacher/one student methods
Programmed learning
Individually prescribed instruction
Personalized system of instruction
Audio--tutorial methods
Distance learning techniques
Resource--based learning techniques
Packaged learning methods
Computer--assisted and computer--managed methods
Systems which integrate "traditional" methods with a variety
    of media or resource--based material
And other techniques (e.g., self--testing)(4)

The obvious way for librarians to learn such techniques is by attendance at courses, but, as we have already seen, it is often very difficult for them to attend such courses. The conclusions drawn from this project, therefore, were that, if the normal type of short course or seminar is not meeting the need which clearly exists, then some other format must be devised. If the librarians cannot come to the courses, then the courses must go out to them. The format which is being developed now is that of a teaching package.

Package on Teaching and Learning Methods for Librarians

The project to develop a package for teaching and learning methods for librarians evolved directly out of this earlier project on the librarians' teaching and learning needs. Again it is funded by the British Library Research and Development Department and based at the University of Surrey, with Dr. P.J. Hills as director, and a working party consisting of representatives of the Polytechnic of North London, South Bank Polytechnic and the University of Surrey, with Mr. Bob Elliott, on sabbatical leave from the University of Windsor, Ontario, as coordinator.

First of all, I must emphasize that the package was not conceived as an equal alternative to one of the courses which I have already described; rather it was felt to be something which could be substituted for a course when financial, administrative or other reasons prevented the user education librarian from attending a course on teaching.

Obviously, one of the main disadvantages of a package over a course where there are live supervisors present is that the practical work must be omitted. If one attends a course, one has the opportunity to play with different bits of equipment, deliver a lecture, prepare an audio tape or tape/slide, and have expert assistance, comment and criticism at the same time. One could perhaps define the aims of the ideal course as providing three elements:

1. information about the state of the art of user education, the theory, the teaching methods in use

2. motivation and encouragement

3. skills

The package can provide only the first, or at most the first two, of these: information and motivation, but not skills. It is essentially passive, not active, learning.

Now to the package itself. As it stands at the moment, it is still very much a trial version. Since the summer of 1977 the working party has been involved in detailed discussions of the form it should take, what types of material it should include, what it should try to teach, and so on. By the spring of this year it had evolved into the form which is illustrated in Appendix 2, and it was ready for the first tests. A pre-pilot test was run at the University of Surrey in February 1978. This was intended mainly to get preliminary reactions from librarians before the main pilot-tests. It was a fairly superficial test, in that the subject librarians at Surrey were given the whole package to work through in a single day and were then asked for their comments. It is interesting, however, that the comments closely resembled those from the librarians attending later pilots.

The main pilot tests took place over a period of two weeks in April 1978. They were held in three libraries in London, the Polytechnic of North London, Middlesex Polytechnic and Bedford College, which is a part of London University. London was chosen simply for geographical convenience, and when the second pilot test is held it will include libraries over a wider geographical area.

When the results of these pilot tests have been finally analyzed, it is possible that major changes will be made to the package. Today, of course, I can only talk to you about the package in the form in which it is at the moment. But I will try to give you an idea of the comments which were made on each section of the package so that you can see how it is likely to change.

The intention is that the package should be used by the librarian in his own library, as and when time permits. For this reason, each of the six parts has been devised so that they can be used independently of each other, in any order, or indeed so that some of them can be omitted altogether if they are not felt to be relevant to that librarian's particular needs.

Part one deals with the general situation of teaching and learning in higher education -- not just in the context of libraries. It consists of two audio tapes, the first a survey of the various teaching methods in use at present, the second a short talk giving advice on how to present a lecture. The remainder of this section consists of notes to accompany the tapes and reprints of articles on teaching and learning theory. This was the section of the package most criticized by the librarians who took part in the pilot tests. They felt that most of it was not relevant to them; typical of the comments were: "too much jargon," "too academic," "too theoretical." It is quite likely, therefore, that this section will have to be completely re-thought and perhaps much of it discarded.

Parts two to six are all accompanied by a set of introductory notes prepared by the working party. Part two surveys the present situation in the United Kingdom as far as teaching methods in libraries are concerned. The lecture is still the most common method employed, generally for "orientation" rather than "instruction." Normally it is used in conjunction with other methods, such as the overhead projector, slides or the chalk board. Seminars and tutorials are common, especially for giving instruction in particular subjects or on particular reference tools. Programmed learning is not used at all. Among audio-visual aids, the overhead projector, the audio tape and the tape/slide are the most popular. The tape/slide is particularly successful as an orientation program, though people seem to be getting more sceptical about its value as an instructional device. The tour is, of course, also widely used in orientation. Practical work is not widespread, mainly because the preparation requires a great deal of time. When it is used, however, it is felt to be very effective, and the working party suggests that if "prepackaged" practical work were available (perhaps something along the lines of the UCLA workbook(7)) practical work might well be more popular. This section also mentions the Travelling Workshops Experiment, based at Newcastle-upon-Tyne Polytechnic, which is essentially an experiment in producing a mixed-media package, initially in three subjects: biology, social welfare and mechanical engineering. On the whole, the librarians felt that this section was useful, because it was practical and relevant.

Part three discusses objectives and evaluation. In dealing with objectives it refers the user to two printed items, the first a British Library report called *Evaluation of Tape-Slide Guides for Library Instruction*.(8) In spite of its title, chapter two of this report covers teaching objectives in general in the library instruction field, and chapter four covers evaluation in the same way. The second reference is to the ACRL guidelines for bibliographic instruction.(9) As far as evaluation is concerned, the working party say that they

> would have liked to offer you a model evaluation scheme. We cannot unfortunately do that . . . . To date very few libraries in the UK, or elsewhere, have taken evaluation seriously, which probably accounts for the high mortality rate amongst many programmes.

I am just going to quote one librarian's comment on this section and leave you to decide whether you agree with her. She said:

> It gives the (correct) impression that truly objective or "scientific" evaluation is well-nigh impossible. Its treatment of evaluation as a theoretical topic does not help the librarian involved in user education who wants some real indications of whether he/she is wasting his/her time.

Part four deals with audio–visual media. The rationale for using AV is given in a quotation from Donald Bligh's book *What's the Use of Lectures?*:

> Films, CCTV and a different speaker on audio–tapes introduced at well–spaced intervals may . . . improve student attention. The BBC varies the form of presentation almost every minute during news and documentary broadcasts, and while it is not to be expected that new lecturers will achieve BBC standards when preparing lectures, they should always ask themselves, "How can I vary my presentation?"(10)

As might be expected, most of the items in this section of the package are themselves audio–visual; the compilers tried wherever possible to have instruction in the same medium as that being taught – an audio tape on making an audio tape, a tape/slide on making a tape/slide, and so on. They also included in their notes a warning that before one embarks on the production of any audio–visual aid, one should weigh up carefully whether the likely use will justify the time and money involved. With all the librarians who have worked through the package, this was by far the most popular and successful section, not, I think, so much because it was largely audio–visual as because it was practical and directly relevant to what they wanted to learn. In this section there is a clear advantage in using some form of audio–visual medium (though not necessarily the same medium as that being taught) because examples can then be given of good and bad points, mistakes, things to avoid, such as poor recording technique.

Part five consists of a reprint of the chapter on library guides from my book on reader instruction.(11) This chapter is an analysis of various features of British university library guides and was not intended as a collection of helpful hints on how to compile a guide. From the comments made on this section, I feel that if anything is needed in the package on printed guides, then it needs to be a more basic series of tips and suggestions.

Part six, conclusions and suggestions for further action, discusses ways of improving library instruction. Many of the participants suggested that this section -- or something like it – should replace part one.

Now, briefly, a few general comments which were made about the package. The main criticism of it was that it was too long, that there was too much material in it, particularly reading matter. Linked with this was the view that there were too many theoretical items and that most, if not all, of these could be discarded. The items which were practical and relevant were, however, liked by most of the participants in the pilot tests. There was some un-- certainty about the exact purpose of the package -- a valid criticism because there is no clear statement of objectives in it. Some librarians were unsure whether it was intended as a self--study scheme, which one would work through from start to finish, or whether it was meant to be a pool of ideas from which the librarian could draw whatever was appropriate to his needs at the time.

As to whether the whole concept of a teaching package is valid, there was no clear view. On the whole it was agreed that most librarians do not, or cannot, attend such few courses as there are available, and that in any case, as these are often not geared specifi-- cally to their requirements, they are often not very relevant for them. There is a need, therefore, for some other means of training the librarian to teach, and the concept of a package is certainly one worth experimenting with.

Handbook for University Lecturers

I am now going to look at a different approach to the problem, the problem being this time not so much the training of librarians as the training of university teachers. This is a series of booklets called *Teaching in Higher Education: Suggestions for the Con-- sideration of Lecturers and Others Concerned with Teaching in Higher Education*.(12) It is the result of a three--year project fi-- nanced by the University Grants Committee at the School of Educa-- tion of the University of Lancaster. Whilst it is aimed mainly at lecturers much of the information it includes is relevant to the teacher--librarian.

The first six of the nine booklets are concerned with different teaching methods, in an essentially practical manner. Let me quote a few examples from book one, called *Lecturecraft*:

> Experience suggests that new lecturers put in too much . . . . There is some evidence that a person may be able to process only 7 ± 2 chunks of information in his mind at any one time.

> There is a limit to the amount of information that can be packed into a lecture and a strong case for using other methods of pre-- senting much of it.

> Lecturers *do* balance on the backs of chairs, poke fingers in their ears, jig about, juggle with chalk, sketch things in the air, mutter, sway hypnotically from foot to foot, put their glasses on and off (heard of bifocals?), lecture with their heads in their hands throughout, jingle their change, fall off the platform, etc. etc.

Their fame liveth for evermore in anecdote.

And so on.

Books two to six discuss the choice of teaching method -- how to choose the most appropriate method of getting your information across, what can best be taught in small groups, what is most suited to audio–visual media. And then, having chosen *how* you want to teach, you are given advice on the ways of handling these different techniques: group management, group behavior, patterns of small group teaching, the individual in the group, the tutor in the group, etc.

The teacher--librarian in Britain, then, who wants to learn how to teach is left very much to his own devices. There are courses for university lecturers which, theoretically, he can attend -- though in practice very few librarians have actually been on such a course. There are short courses for librarians, but these are mainly concerned with audio–visual media, not with teaching methods as such. Often there are financial or administrative difficulties which prevent the librarian from attending such courses. The Surrey teaching package is being developed in an attempt to overcome these difficulties, and to take the courses to the librarian in his own library. And perhaps by the end of the conference I might have some further ideas to take back across the Atlantic.

REFERENCES

1. Review Committee on Education for Information Use, *Final report*. (British Library Research and Development Report 5325.) London: British Library, 1977.

2. Hammond, Nancy, "Teaching and learning methods for British librarians." In: *Putting library instruction in its place*. Ann Arbor: Pierian, 1978.

3. Roberts, N. (ed.), *Education, training and the use of staff: summary proceedings of a one-day forum on the educational and training implications of the Sheffield Manpower Project*. (British Library Research and Development Report 5394.) Sheffield: Postgraduate School of Librarianship and Information Science, 1977.

4. Hills, P.J., *Librarians' needs in relation to teaching and learning methods in higher education*. (Forthcoming British Library Research and Development Report.)

5. Available from: Ian Malley, British Library Information Officer for User Education, University of Technology, Loughborough, Leicestershire, LE11 3TU, England.

6. Available from: Dr. R.G. Lester, The Library, Queen Elizabeth College, Campden Hill Road, London, W8 7AH, England.

7. Dudley, Miriam, *Workbook in library skills: a self-directed course in the use of UCLA's College Library*. Los Angeles: University of California Library, 1973.

8. Hills, P.J., Lincoln, L. and Turner, L.P., *Evaluation of tape/slide guides for library education*. (British Library Research and Development Report 5378.) Guildford: University of Surrey, 1978.

9. American College and Research Libraries, Bibliographic Instruction Section, "Towards guidelines for bibliographic instruction in academic libraries," *College and research libraries news*, 36 (3) May 1975, 137--139 and 169--171.

10. Bligh, D.A., *What's the use of lectures?* 3rd ed. Harmondsworth: Penguin, 1972.

11. Fox, Peter, *Reader instruction methods in academic libraries, 1973*, Cambridge: University Library, 1974.

12. *Teaching in higher education series: suggestions for the consideration of lecturers and others concerned with teaching in higher education.* Lancaster: School of Education, University of Lancaster, 1978.
    By Barbara Cockburn and Alec Ross:
        Vol. 1: *Lecturecraft*
        Vol. 2: *Why lecture?*
        Vol. 3: *Working together*
        Vol. 4: *Participatory discussion*
        Vol. 5: *A kind of learning*
        Vol. 6: *Patterns and procedures*
        Vol. 7: *Inside assessment*
        Vol. 8: *Essays*
    By John Matthews:
        Vol. 9: *The use of objective tests*

APPENDIX 1: COURSE IN TEACHING AND LEARNING IN HIGHER EDUCATION 1978

	0900–1015 coffee	1045–1200	lunch 1330–1500	tea 1530–1800	supper	1930–2100
Wed 13 Sept			(Note) 1430–1530 REGISTRATION	(Note) 1600–1745 INTRODUCTION	Meet Group Tutors	Stills, Film and Television (L)
Thurs 14 Sept	Making TV Tape Making Tape/Slide (L)	On Lecturing (L)	On Lecturing (D)	Practice Lecture (W) Educational Aids (W) TV/Tape/Slide (W) Group Activity (W)		Self Teaching (L)
Fri 15 Sept	Student Learning (LD)		Aims and Curriculum Development (L)	Practice Lecture (W) Educational Aids (W) TV/Tape/Slide (W) Group Activity (W)		PARTY
Sat 16 Sept	FREE	Assessment and Examinations (L)	Assessment and Examinations (D)	Practice Lecture (W) Educational Aids (W) TV/Tape/Slide (W) Group Activity (W)		Lecture Playback (W) Group Case Studies (W)
Sun 17 Sept	FREE		Small Group Teaching (L)	Small Group Teaching (W)		Lecture Playback (W) Practice Small Grps Group Case Studies (W)
Mon 18 Sept	Study Counselling (LD)		Evaluation (L)	Practice Small Groups (W) Educational Aids (W) TV/Tape/Slide (W) Group Activity (W)		Keller Plan (W) or Objective Testing (W) or Evaluation (W)
Tues 19 Sept	Practice Lecture (W) Educational Aids (W) TV/Tape/Slide (W) Group Activity (W)		Math for non-mathematicians or (L) Laboratory Aims (L) or Practice Small Groups (W)	Practice Lecture (W) Educational Aids (W) TV/Tape/Slide (W) Group Activity (W)		Workshop Preparation Time
Wed 20 Sept	Simulation (W)		Review of Group Activities (In groups) (D)	Keller Plan (W) or Objectives Testing (W) or Evaluation (W)		Showing of Group TV and Tape/Slide

Appendix 1, continued

NOTES ON TIMETABLE

Abbreviations

(L) = Lecture or Seminar
(D) = General Discussion
(W) = Workshop

1. The course participants will be divided into six groups, and the actual composition of the groups will be decided by the tutors when all applications have been received. Certain activities on the course are kept separate for Science groups, others for Arts groups. Other activities do allow for some individual choice. Some groups will produce a teaching videotape, while others will produce a tape/slide presentation for teaching purposes. Preferences should be stated on the application form. As far as possible we will try to accommodate them.

2. The course in very intensive. This is essential to provide a really worthwhile course in the time available. Previous participants have expressed a preference for such an intensive course.

3. Although the course is very intensive, some private study time is available, including Sunday morning. It may be possible to arrange visits to local places of interest if required. We hope that all participants will come to the Party on Friday evening, which is an important part of the course!

4. Overseas participants are welcome; but we must emphasize that fluent command of English is essential if participants are to profit from and contribute to in--depth discussion.

5. If you have any questions about the time-table, please get in touch with:
    Miss D. Gray
    IET
    University of Surrey
    Tel: 0483--71281, Ext. 619

APPENDIX 2

A PACKAGE ON TEACHING AND LEARNING METHODS FOR LIBRARIANS

Introduction and List of Contents

The purpose of this package is to provide librarians with information on the range of teaching and learning methods being used in higher education, in the context of user education. By "user education" is meant all issues concerned with library orientation and instruction, ranging from the orientation tour to the more advanced aspects of literature searching.

The package was designed for librarians who find it difficult to find time to attend a formal course in teaching and learning methods. The package consists of six parts: the first five parts acquaint librarians with various teaching methods and related issues; the sixth, and final, part summarizes the package and also suggests follow-up activities which actively involve the librarians with material covered in the package.

The List of Contents attached to this introduction describes each part, so that you can decide which to use, and in what order. It is not necessary to make use of everything in the package. What might prove helpful to you will depend on your own interest and experience. Covering one item may lead to curiosity about another.

This is a trial version of the package. When you have completed it, you will be asked to fill out a written evaluation of the package as a whole.

List of Contents

The package is divided into six parts. They do not necessarily have to be used in total, or in sequence.

Part 1: "Teaching and Learning in Higher Education"

Contents
1.1   One 20 minute audio-tape on "Teaching and Learning in Higher Education" by Phil Hills.

Appendix 2, continued

1.2 One typescript on "Teaching and Learning in Higher Education" by Phil Hills, which supplements the audio–tape.

1.3 One audio–tape (9 minutes) on "The Lecture – Aims and Skills" by Prof. Lewis Elton, Head of the Institute for Educational Technology, University of Surrey.

1.4 One typescript on "The Lecture – Some Precepts," which supplements the audio–tape 1.3.

1.5 Reprint of article: Postlethwait, S.N. "Teaching Tools and Techniques; An Audio–tutorial Approach to Teaching." *Pacific Speech.* Vol. 1, No. 4, pp57–62, 1966.
   This article gives:
   1. the history of the audio–tutorial system, p57;
   2. some early results, p58;
   3. some important aspects of the system, p60.

1.6 Reprint of article: Keller, Fred. "Goodbye Teacher . . . " *Journal of Applied Behaviour Analysis.* Vol. 1, No. 1, Spring 1968, pp79–89.
   This is the original article on the Keller Plan. Page 83 gives an early account of the method describing its essential features.

1.7 Reprint of article: Bridge, Will. "Self–study Courses in Undergraduate Science Teaching; The Report of a Survey." *Higher Education.* Vol. 5, 1976, pp211–224.
   This paper surveys the use of self–study courses in universities, polytechnics and colleges in the U.K. and Ireland.

1.8 Reprint of article: Davis, Q.V. and Hills, P.J. "The Application of a Systematic Approach to an Electrical Engineering Course." In *Aspects of Educational Technology VI* (Ed. by Austwick, K. and Harris, N.D.C.). Pitman Publishing, London, 1972.
   This article describes the system on page 185. Results obtained in a first year electrical engineering course are given on page 188 onwards.

1.9 Reprint of article: Goldschmid, B. and Goldschmid, M. "Individualising Instruction in Higher Education: A Review." *Higher Education.* Vol. 3, 1973, pp1–24.
   This article ranges over a variety of approaches to individual approaches. Modular instruction is described on page 6.

1.10 Reprint of article: Hooper, R. and Toye, I. (eds.), *Computer Assisted Learning in the United Kingdom; Some Case Studies.* London: Councils and Education Press Ltd., 1975.

Appendix 2, continued

>ppIX–XXIX.
>This paper gives:
>1. a definition of terms, page IX;
>2. a variety of uses for computers, pages X–XIII;
>3. the state of the art in the U.K. as of 1973/4, page XIV onwards.

Part 2: *"Teaching Methods and User Education Programmes: The Present Situation"*

Contents
2.1   A set of notes by the Working Party which outlines what teaching methods are being used, and not used, in U.K. user education programmes.
2.2   Reprint of article: Fjallbrant, N. "Teaching Methods for the Education of the Library User." *Libri*. Vol. 26, No. 4, 1976, pp252–267.
>A very good survey article for anyone who wants more information than what was outlined in the notes (item 2.1). It also has a valuable bibliography.

Part 3: *"Objectives and Evaluation in Relation to Teaching Methods"*

Contents
3.1   A set of notes on the topic by the Working Party
3.2   Reprint of article: Harris, C. "Illuminative Evaluation of User Education Programmes." *Aslib Proceedings*. Vol. 29, No. 10, October 1977, pp348–362.
3.3   Reprint of article: Brewer, J.G. and Hills, P.J. "Evaluation of Reader Instruction." *Libri*. Vol. 26, No. 1, 1976, pp55–65.
>Good survey of the whole area, if one wants to go beyond the Working Party's notes.

Part 4: *"Teaching with Audio–visual Materials"*

Contents
4.1   A set of notes on the topic by the Working Party
4.2   Reprint of chapter: Jay, A. "Visual Aids and the Use of Pictures." In *Effective Presentation*. London: British Institute of Management, 1976.
4.3   Reprint of article: Cowen, J. "How to Choose Between Modes of Pre–recording Instruction by Using Utterly Selfish

Appendix 2, continued

	Criteria." Ontario Universities Program for Instructional Development, *Newsletter*. No. 16, May 1977.
4.4	Two tape/slide packages on how to make your own tape/
4.5	slide.
	The Working Party was unable to decide which one would be the most effective in this situation; we would welcome comments as to which one you feel is the most effective. 4.4 is by Ann Irving (Liverpool Polytechnic Library) and 4.5 is by Roy Adams (Trent Polytechnic Library).
4.6	One audio–tape on how to use audio–tape. By Tom Evans, School of Librarianship, Aberystwyth, Wales.
4.7	One video–tape on how to make an effective video–tape. By Pat Wisher, City of London Polytechnic.
4.8	10 minute tape/slide on the Use of the Overhead Projector. By David Uzzell, Psychology Department, University of Surrey.

Part 5: "Teaching with Printed Materials"

Contents

5.1	A set of notes on the topic by the Working Party.
5.2	Reprint of a chapter: Fox, P. "Guidance in Printed Form." In *Reader Instruction Methods in Academic Libraries*. Cambridge University Library (Librarianship Series No. 1). 1974.
	Extremely good overview of many academic use printed publications in their user education programme.

Part 6: "Conclusions and Suggestions for Further Action"

Contents

6.1	Brief summary of the first five parts of the Package.
6.2	Suggestions for further action: Using the materials in the first five parts of the package was a fairly passive learning experience. What is suggested in this section of the package are activities which librarians can do, activities related to their user education programme.
6.3	LIMB (Library Instruction Materials Bank). If you are interested in obtaining information about what library instruction materials are in use at other libraries, contact LIMB.

Appendix 2, continued

Conclusion

In Part One of this package you were given information about important teaching methods in use today in higher education. The methods were chosen because of their possible relevance to a user education program. Phil Hills described teaching methods which can be effective with individual, or small groups, of students. With the exception of package learning, very few of these techniques he described are used in any known user education program; but they could be. Lewis Elton's description of the lecture method demonstrated that the lecture does not have to be passive; the lecture audience can be encouraged to participate to some degree. In short, there are many teaching methods in higher education which could be, with some adaptation, applied to a user education program.

Part Two of the package outlined teaching methods which are presently in use in user education programs. The most popular methods are apparently some form of lecture, printed handouts, the traditional tour, and, the most recent innovation, the tape/slide package. To a limited degree, there is some overlapping between teaching methods as discussed in Part One and Part Two. Thus, librarians are using and experimenting with teaching methods which are used in higher education in general.

Part Three presented the issues of objectives and evaluation. The quality and quantity of the material taught has a very strong influence on what teaching methods are used and to what degree they are successful.

Lastly, in Parts Four and Five, audio-visual and printed materials were covered. Most teaching today relies on some form of printed and audio-visual materials. In fact, most teaching uses a mixed-media approach (e.g., the lecture and the overhead projector, handout, etc.).

To what extent the information offered in Parts One through Five of this package is relevant to your job determines the package's usefulness. Does the package offer librarians, who cannot attend courses, adequate information on how to improve their teaching skills? How can the package be improved in the future, in terms of modifications, in order to be more effective? It is questions such as these that will have to be answered before a permanent package on teaching methods for librarians can be constructed.

Appendix 2, continued

Suggestions for Further Action

Suggestion One: "Find out who can help"

When making teaching plans for a user education program, take advantage of expert help from inside and outside the library. For example, if planning library instruction for a political science class, ask the government documents librarian, or someone with similar talents, to put together a handout or audio–visual presentation on documents and their use.

This also applies to potential help from outside the library. Many campuses, for instance, have some sort of audio–visual unit. Find out what services this unit offers, and get the names of the various experts within the unit, e.g., people responsible for graphics, still–photography, audio– and video–tape, etc.

Do not be shy about asking for help.

Suggestion Two: "Improve your library's orientation program"

Using some of the methods and techniques mentioned in this package, try your hand at developing an orientation project. For example, a printed self–guided tour could be produced. Consult other library staff members to find out what they think should be included; consult a printer to see how feasible the idea is in terms of materials and costs; and, most importantly, consult students by showing them a rough draft of the tour and asking for their candid impressions.

No matter what idea you choose to develop, pick something which will attempt to change the students' attitude towards the library. An orientation project's first aim is to encourage students to use the library without fear and trepidation.

Suggestion Three: "Improve library instruction"

This could be accomplished by planning a library instruction unit which can be integrated into an established subject course. Such an experiment could be undertaken by these steps:
1. Pick a course and find out from the instructor what assignments are required, e.g., term papers, essays, or anything else which requires some form of research which goes beyond lecture notes and textbooks.
2. After having determined the students' needs, ask yourself how the library could best help; what teaching methods would be most useful, e.g., practical work, printed information guides, tape/slide presentation, etc.

Appendix 2, continued

> 3. make arrangements with the course's instructor to teach a library instruction unit in his class.

If it works, you will have made a friend, and convert, in a teaching department. That encounter could lead to more contacts with other instructors because of the successful precedent.

Suggestion Four: "Keep in touch with user education developments"

At this time, probably the best way of doing this in the U.K. is by reading *Infuse*, and knowing that you can use the expertise of the British Library's Information Officer for User Education. *Infuse* is published by this same officer. Via this newsletter the officer keeps U.K. librarians in touch with developments in user education. For more information about *Infuse*, or the officer, contact:

Ian Malley
Information Officer for User Education
Library
University of Technology
Loughborough, Leicestershire. LE11 3TU.

Suggestion Five: "Try to attend some form of post-experience course work on teaching and learning methods"

More and more teaching methods courses are being developed and offered in the U.K. Although this package is useful in terms of introducing you to teaching and learning methods, it is not a total replacement for a teaching and learning course.

LIMB (Library Instruction Materials Bank)

Ian Malley, British Library Information Officer for User Education, has recently set up a Library Instruction Materials Bank. The text below is his description of this new service:

A wide range of print and non-print material is used in association with user education. A Library Instruction Materials Bank (LIMB) has now been set up by the British Library Information Officer for User Education at Loughborough University of Technology. All producers of relevant material from all types of libraries in the United Kingdom are asked to deposit ten copies of each item (except audiovisual materials) with LIMB. The range of print materials is as follows:

Appendix 2, continued

Audio--visual aids guides	Manuscripts guides
Books guides	Microforms guides
Catalogue guides	Patents guides
Charts	Periodicals guides
Classification guides	Programmed instruction
Computer–assisted programs	Publicity materials
Courses outlines	Reference books guides
Evaluation forms	Reports guides
Exercises	Research guides
Faculty cooperation information	Research proposals
Floor plans	Services guides
Government publications guides	Standards guides
Indexes and abstracts guides	Subject guides
Lecture outlines	Teaching handouts
Library guides	Tests
Library (faculty) guides	Theses guides
Locator guides	Tours
	Trade literature guides

In response to enquiries about the availability of certain types of material, the enquirer will in the first place be sent a printout with details of relevant material held in LIMB. The enquirer having noted what is most relevant can either write back to LIMB or write to the producing library for the materials. There is no charge for the service and it is accessible to anyone with an interest in user education.

PROJECT LOEX AND THE NATIONAL SCENE

Carolyn Kirkendall
Director, Project LOEX
Center of Educational Resources
Eastern Michigan University

To begin this year's report from the national LOEX office, I would like to say a very grateful Thank You for supporting the clearinghouse with your letters, your contributions of materials for our collection, for your encouragement, and particularly for sending in your membership/subscription fees. Thanks to your support, we will continue to provide LOEX exchange services throughout 1978.

As earlier reported, our present grant funding is expiring. While we are seeking additional support, we are also attempting to become a financially self–sustaining agency. Due to your monetary en–couragement, we are doing just that, and there could be no other way to begin a LOEX report than by expressing my gratitude to those of you who have paid for this initial year of service.

Interest in bibliographic instruction, I'm happy to report, con–tinues to grow. The most evident proof of this growth from our central vantagepoint is that people and libraries are willing to pay to borrow sample materials and receive news of the field.

Today's LOEX report is intended to bring Conference attendees up–to–date on current trends in the field of academic library in–struction:

— our national LOEX agency is now in contact with some 1,600 academic libraries who are establishing or maintaining some sort of library orientation/instruction activity. This number has grown from exactly 258 libraries three years ago at Conference time.

— you are no doubt aware of the growth in the number of meetings, conferences, workshops, and seminars on instruc–tion which are being scheduled and held across the country – more and more each season.

— the number of journal articles related to bibliographic instruction has doubled over the past year, as a check of *Library Literature*, other indexes, and the bibliography you will find in your registration packet reveals. In addition, 19% of these articles are concerned with subject--related instruction or were published in discipline--related journals of higher education other than library--related publications.

— more than 25 local, state and regional clearinghouses on library instruction, as well as various national committees, are now in operation. These clearinghouse agencies publish newsletters, issue directories, and sponsor regionally located workshops.

— besides the national U.S. exchange, Project LOEX, there are now also national offices in the United Kingdom, Scandinavia, and Australia.

— you may have noticed that many, many more reference and public service job descriptions listed in the "help wanted" sections of *American Libraries* and the *C&RL News* include the terms "orientation," "instruction," or "user education experience" as requirements of the posted position. In fact, about 70% of all these public services advertisements in the past two years include these terms. This may mean (although we cannot tell without eavesdropping) that library directors are actually querying prospective librarians as to their experience in and commitment to instruction.

— some library schools continue to include instruction as part of their curricula, due, in part, to demand from the field -- from new librarians who discover they should have had some training and exposure to library use teaching before confronting the need for it, and providing solutions to this need.

— instruction has been officially recognized through the American Library Association with its newly--established Library Instruction Round Table and the ACRL Bibliographic Instruction Section.

— a revised edition of *Educating the Library User*, a basic introduction to library instruction, edited by John Lubans, will be published this year.

— commercial publishers are taking an interest in producing workbooks, exercises, textbooks and a--v tools related to our field, as they recognize they could tap a great potential market.

— grant funding for instruction programs – though its status is somewhat tenuous from current reports -- has definitely expanded in the past two years, with 26 Library Service Enhancement Programs awarded by the Council on Library Resources and continuing College Library Program grants by CLR/NEH. Evidence of increasing local grant funding is apparent, fortunately, as institutions seem to recognize that the role of their reference librarians can also be that of teachers.

— some sort of completed exercise or assignment in library skills is being required of students in more institutions – either for graduation (a rarity) or for a unit of credit within a required course.

— the number of credit courses in library skills is still expand-- ing, particularly those courses utilizing self--paced methods, with the library staff providing the guidance.

— separate divisions, departments and committees of instruc- tion also continue to be established within academic library structures, because of the need to coordinate the instruction activity. Also expanding is the number of library staff posi- tions with sole responsibility for coordinating and/or con- ducting the instruction projects.

All of these areas seem to be good, healthy indicators that bibliographic instruction should be here to stay, that a public ser- vice job does indeed include the responsibility for education, that instruction is no more a "trend" or an "issue" (as Joe Boissé told us here last year) than are interlibrary loan or circulation trends or issues.

At the LOEX office, we are most often asked to respond to this question: which are the best methods and techniques to use in academic library instruction today? And the answer remains the same: any well–thought out and well–prepared method will work if it serves the library patrons at the point and time of their needs.

Currently popular methods during the past year appear to be: point--of--use a--v tools, printed self–guided tours, self–paced exer- cises and workbooks, discipline--related handouts, pretests to determine students' lack of skills, and the development of uniform systems of library signs to implement the instruction.

Most successful programs now have administrative backing of some sort. While almost all existing programs in the United States have developed from the grass-roots level through the energetic dedication of one enthusiastic individual, once the philosophy of providing instruction as a necessary service gains momentum, and once responsibilities are distributed and the program becomes more formally organized, the more secure the program becomes. The library at this stage need no longer rely on the personality and energies of one person to assure the success of a program.

What is needed for a good program, in part, is enthusiasm, a well-thought-out project, a little time stolen away from the reference desk, some staff and faculty support, a little creativity, and a few -- not many -- funds. Instruction itself is not just a frill, or a public relations ploy to lure students into the building, or a gimmick for exposure, or a convenient bandwagon onto which the ambitious reference librarian can jump to be seen. It is an essential service of the academic library.

As such, a good program cannot continue unless the users benefit from and recognize the value of their instruction experience. This means libraries should measure, by some means, the value of the activity they offer, that they should remain flexible in order to change the objectives of their projects as the needs of the patrons change, and that they ought to begin with some sort of long-range plan in mind. This planning ought also to involve the library, staff and the faculty, and would benefit from an initial user assessment survey. Once the activity is initiated, there ought to be an attempt to develop a testing instrument to gauge the project's effectiveness on users -- whether they retain what's been taught, whether the faculty notices any improvement in students' skills, whether the library itself is affected, and how, and to what extent, whether the instruction activity has saved instructional time or created more work, and, if it's the latter, whether this work is necessary or helpful or overwhelming.

Library user education programs in colleges and universities today seem to be maintaining a very high level. Hopefully, this concept will not (as it has cyclically done in the past) diminish in importance, but will remain a legitimate and permanent part of the library's work. The faculty, the students and the library itself benefit from such organized and formally established activity. The role of the library is not only enhanced, but instruction directly influences the library to become what it ought to be in higher education today -- a real, integral and indispensable part of the instructional process.

IMPLEMENTING INSTRUCTIONAL METHODS: A PANEL

Katherine Rottsolk, Moderator
Reference Librarian
St. Olaf College

The fascination I find at a LOEX conference is that of sharing a common goal with everyone here, that goal of, in Bonnie Frick's words, "developing intelligent persons who, independently, can locate and assess the sources of information needed for a wide variety of intellectual, social and personal concerns," and then learning about the various routes we are taking to reach that goal.

The panelists today will emphasize approaches which adapt best to the situation in their particular institutions. I look forward to hearing them so that some of their ideas which have been proved workable can be adapted for St. Olaf's programs. One of the most important things I gain from a LOEX conference is the chance to listen to, talk with, and look over the materials of librarians who have emphasized a different instructional approach from ours. Usually I find something in each that might work for us better than something we are now doing.

At St. Olaf College, our evolving program makes no claim to be other than derivative. We have no plans to reinvent the wheel; we just adjust the air pressure in the tires to make for a smoother ride. I hope other librarians are flattered when we adapt their ideas or their materials to our unique institutional needs. We do try to acknowledge our indebtedness; "freely adapted from . . . " is sprinkled liberally through our assignment--specific search strategies and limited bibliographies.

Let me give you a brief summary of the evolution of the library instruction program at St. Olaf, an undergraduate, chiefly residential, liberal arts college of about 2900 students, 190 faculty and five (now six) professional librarians. Over the past 20 years our acquisitions have been carefully chosen so that, although our book budget is limited, it has been extraordinarily well--managed. Parenthetically, I do not know how one could begin an instruction program without adequate reference materials and without access to a good share of the identified subject matter, both books and periodical articles. Even with our substantial book collection and with borrowing privileges at Carleton College, only a mile away, I doubt that we could have undertaken our present program were it not for MINITEX, the statewide Minnesota interlibrary loan service.

At any rate, we had been slowly building our library instruction program in the traditional manner, through personal contacts and persistence, but there seemed to be no way to make it campus-wide. Still, we agreed with Patricia Knapp when she said, "If librarians want to reach the vast majority of undergraduate students, they must work with and through the teaching faculty to ensure that use of the library is a required, essential component in course work."

The foundations were sound, the materials collection was acceptable, the staff was of one mind as to the importance of library instruction, but we were still fumbling, trying to figure out what would work for us -- and we couldn't run the risk of too many failures as we built up the program.

Then things began to fall into place. First, I was awarded a Council on Library Resources fellowship which allowed me, on my sabbatical, to visit and work with the librarians, faculty, and students in several colleges known to have successful library instruction programs, ranging from the traditional to the more experimental. Then a biology professor and I made up one of the teams attending the first NSF Workshop on Course-Related Library and Literature Use Instruction in Undergraduate Science Education held at Earlham -- wonderfully helpful! And, finally, St. Olaf was awarded one of the 5-year College Library Program grants. Jointly funded by the Council on Library Resources and the National Endowment for the Humanities, it requires matching funds from the local institution. That was important for us because it gave visibility and importance to our library instruction program on the campus, and we needed that.

If, at St. Olaf, our program is unique at all, it is in our emphasis on a team approach – a team that includes all the librarians, a faculty advisory committee, and student assistants. All were or have become converts to the expressed goal of a sequential program of library instruction in which we identify library skills -- both knowledge of tools and of research methods peculiar to the subject area – and then address those needs by working closely with classroom instructors. Together we plan assignments which meet both the course objectives and the overall library instruction objectives. Working with this broad representation of campus groups, we hope that our program will be relatively free from the dependence upon one individual's activities; that it, instead, will become an essential component of each department's curriculum.

REFERENCES

Frick, Elizabeth. "Information Structure and Bibliographic Instruction." JAL 1975, pp12--14.

Patricia Knapp in a paper, "The Library, the Undergraduate, and the Teaching Faculty," given at the Institute on Training for Librarians in Undergraduate Libraries held at the University of California in San Diego, August 17--21, 1970, p12.

THE FRESHMAN INSTRUCTION PROGRAM
AT THE UNIVERSITY OF ILLINOIS
UNDERGRADUATE LIBRARY

Melissa Cain
Assistant Undergraduate Librarian
University of Illinois
Urbana

There are three fundamental aims in teaching library use to the freshman student at the University of Illinois Undergraduate Library. These are: 1) to introduce the student to the intricacies of a complex and large library system (which includes thirty-five departmental libraries as well as the general stacks collection of over 3½ million books); 2) to ensure that the freshman student can understand and use the most important reference works and library tools; and 3) to create, from the beginning, a positive attitude towards the use of the library and to help alleviate fear, negativity and frustration. Though these aims are not novel, it is important for this discussion to restate the fundamental purposes of orientation and instruction.

The methods used in reaching the freshman student are traditional in that we attempt to contact all entering freshman students through a cooperative effort with the faculties of the Rhetoric and Speech Communications departments who are instructing freshmen. (Each year the University of Illinois at Urbana has an entering freshman class of approximately 5,000 students and each student is required to enroll in either a Rhetoric or Speech course.) The instructional programs in the Undergraduate Library are not directed only to the freshmen but the freshmen have been a priority. This clientele is important to us because we are an Undergraduate Library and because many departmental libraries do not focus their instructional efforts at this level. Every freshman student at Illinois is required to embark upon a research project -- which culminates in a 10--12 page "term paper." The Rhetoric Department to date has held firm on this requirement. There are no immediate indications that this will change. Therefore, we must design a program that allows for the best possible "first" research experience in the library and one that will result in the students viewing the library as an information center, the librarians as information specialists, and above all, as teachers.

In outline, the phases in our instructional program are as follows:
1. Library Tour
2. Library Lecture
3. Work Session
4. Term Paper Counseling

I do not intend to dwell upon the library tour. It is a phase of the program that usually involves the pre-professional academic staff, and seldom involves the professional staff. Self-guided tours are available and with an effective system of signs tours are not always necessary. However, if an instructor requests such a tour it is supplied. The tours include a walk through both the Undergraduate Library and the Main Library. This is valuable from the standpoint that it might well be the only opportunity the freshman student, or the undergraduate, has for admittance to the book stacks. It is important that the undergraduate sees the collection and can visualize what it contains even though the book stacks are "open" only to graduate students and faculty for browsing and retrieval purposes. Otherwise, the stacks remain a mystery from which the undergraduate feels excluded. With the recent development of a slide/tape library orientation program, the library tour is less popular than it once was. Also, during New Student Week the "Illini Guides" (upperclassmen working voluntarily) give new students library tours which often make the formal library tour unnecessary, but sometimes offer misleading information. We do not consider the tour as a vehicle for instructional purposes but rather for orientation.

I will now concentrate on the second, third, and fourth phases of the freshman program -- the library lecture, the work session, and the term paper counseling.

The library lecture is a formal classroom presentation that usually takes one class period -- or one hour. It is scheduled by the instructor. The class convenes in the Undergraduate Library. The library lecture is only offered during the first eight weeks of the term. Instructors are notified of the availability of instruction and informed of the lecture's purpose and content. They are encouraged to bring their classes to the library. Each faculty member receives a personal letter detailing the program, notices appear in the department newsletters, and undergraduate librarians are present to describe the program at faculty meetings.

The library lecture is designed to introduce the student to the card catalog (particularly the unique characteristics of the UI catalog); the Serial Record (another perplexing and difficult tool); periodical and newspaper indexes; the use of microfilm and microfiche; and the potential and availability of on-line search services.

The presentation is supplemented by a slide/tape presentation covering the use of the main card catalog and the shelf list, and also explains how an undergraduate student may access materials located in the book stacks. The lecture stimulates students to learn the use of the entire library system and not to rely solely upon the Undergraduate Library collection. Given the size and complexity of the University of Illinois Library's collection this kind of encouragement is a major responsibility.

The content of the library lecture is designed and up--dated by the undergraduate librarians. The academic staff of graduate assistants is given guidance in how best to present the material and they then give the actual presentation. The lecture is usually not delivered to the student at the exact time of the term paper assignment -- normally it precedes the assignment by one or more weeks. Though this arrangement may not be ideal, the separation is necessary as the size of our academic library staff (four professionals and ten pre--professionals) does not allow for the lecture to be given at the same time as the later phases of the instructional program.

Library lectures are popular with the faculty and students. Our statistics show that nearly two--thirds of all potential faculty schedule lectures. A survey done in the fall of 1977 showed that 99 percent of the participating students felt the information contained in the presentation was relevant to their library use needs; 87 percent felt that the amount of information provided was adequate; and 64 percent wanted further instruction in the use of the library. The majority of students wanting further instruction indicated they would prefer this to be an audio-visual format -- most specifically the slide/tape format -- or through computer--assisted instruction such as PLATO (the University of Illinois computer instruction system). Only 6 percent were interested in a credit course, and only 3 percent expressed interest in a workbook approach. As suggested by these students, additional slide/tape presentations are now being developed by library faculty and media specialists for use in the fall of 1978. Also, the undergraduate librarians have signed on as authors of PLATO to learn to design programmed instruction. A new media center in the Undergraduate Library is scheduled to open then so it will be possible to make these presentations available to the student on an individual, as well as group, basis. We are also exploring the possibilities of making these presentations available in selected departmental libraries in a microfiche format. This will mean that all students, not only freshmen, will have access to the instructional media programs.

The third phase of the freshman instructional program is known as the work session. The purpose of the work session is to offer the instructor and the students the opportunity to begin research in the library under the direct guidance of a librarian or another member of the academic staff. The work session is scheduled once the students have selected their topics for research. The library staff receives a list of topics from each instructor before the meeting with each class. Similar topics are grouped together and participating library staff are asked to prepare suggestions on research strategy for the individual students. The class is divided into small groups of 4--6 students and a librarian or graduate library science student works with the individuals in each group. This approach has certain advantages and disadvantages. The advantages are 1) the instructor is present at the work session enabling immediate and effective communication between the classroom faculty, the library faculty, and the student concerning research problems; 2) the students are required to attend as a course obligation; and 3) student motivation is high as the instruction directly relates to a problem at hand. The disadvantages include: 1) the large number of librarians and preprofessionals required for each session (between 3 and 5 persons are needed for each meeting); 2) students may not be prepared to begin research; and 3) crowded conditions and confusion may result at the catalog and index tables.

Classroom faculty tend to respond favorably to this approach. They are able to witness the actual skills the library faculty possess and the approach to solving problems which is taken with the students. It is common to have an instructor remain at the close of the session and comment on the library staff's breadth and depth of knowledge. The work session offers the librarian the opportunity to demonstrate actively to the classroom instructor that even basic research problems have complexities. The demand for work sessions has diminished somewhat with the advent of term paper counseling.

Term paper counseling is an individualized instructional program. Library faculty (drawn from Technical Services, Public Services, and Library Administration) are requested to participate as counselors. They bring their special subject expertise as well as their general professional knowledge to the freshman student. The counseling service follows the library lecture and generally runs from three to four weeks. The exact time is determined by identifying (in advance) the weeks when the "paper crunch" will occur. This is when the Undergraduate Library is overflowing with students needing direction and the reference staff cannot begin to handle the student demands. It is necessary to have additional support services for the individual.

The counseling service is staffed with professional librarians only. Since the program is a "teaching tutorial" it is essential to have faculty who are familiar with the entire UI Library system, are prepared to make accurate referrals to other departmental

libraries when needed and understand all aspects of librarianship. This service requires a large number of volunteers to be effective. The Undergraduate Library has been successful in recruiting volunteers for term paper counseling even though the counseling involves evening and weekend work and though it involves working in an unfamiliar environment. During the preparatory week for our latest term paper counseling program the participating faculty were asked reasons why they had volunteered. Among the most common replies were:
— to gain experience in reference work
— to apply professional knowledge which is otherwise not used
— out of general interest
— as a result of peer pressure.

It is instructive to see how a progressive and dynamic service such as term paper counseling can engage the interest of a wide range of library faculty. The survey done at Pennsylvania State University (1) showed that librarians unanimously agreed that library instruction was their responsibility. It also found that a high number of librarians were willing to participate, but that this willingness diminished as the level of students needing instruction was raised. It is not surprising, therefore, to discover at the University of Illinois that the Undergraduate Library (with its freshman instruction program) can continue to attract willing help from the faculty. Some departmental or technical service librarians are not able to assume a regular counseling schedule. Often these librarians will volunteer their assistance to the freshman on an appointment basis. They then meet the student in individual libraries or departments for discussion. Each term the Undergraduate Library creates a referral file of such faculty and asks term paper counselors to use it in suggesting further personal assistance for those students needing it. It is the student's responsibility to make the appointment.

Term paper counseling is offered from a desk in the Undergraduate Library near the general reference desk. It is positioned by the catalog, indexes, and also visible from the entrance to the library. Although the desk is clearly marked, students sometimes take their term paper problems to the reference desk. We ask the reference staff to refer these students to the counselors and thereby ensure that the student will have an in-depth, uninterrupted interview. (The average time for a counseling interview is 20 minutes.) The reference staff is then available to work on other queries which may more directly use the reference collection.

Before the counseling starts, a meeting is held for participating faculty in order to 1) orient them to the library; 2) discuss the objectives of the program; 3) make them familiar with instructional materials developed and their use; 4) answer any questions they might have and 5) work out the details of the schedule. This meeting provides the only opportunity for the counselors to meet and discuss the service as a whole.

The counseling service and the work session attempt to reinforce the objectives of effective learning.(2) These are: motivation; activity; feedback; and understanding. The student using the counseling service will be *motivated* by a need to solve a problem, in this case the construction of a preliminary reading list, and the collection of relevant data. The *activity* involves both the student and the librarian in the process of assessing information and in this way the student is an active participant, not a passive recipient. The *interaction* of librarian and student guarantees that the student receives information on his or her progress at each step of the process. In the end, the student has not only gained information but also some *understanding* of the bibliographic process which will enable him or her to garner future knowledge.

The primary student behavioral objectives (briefly stated) of Term Paper Counseling are:
1. To state the topic concisely.
2. To select and locate appropriate indexes.
3. To locate relevant subject headings in the catalog and indexes.
4. To construct a preliminary reading list.
5. To identify relevant classification numbers.
6. To identify specialized departmental libraries for further research; and
7. To ultimately produce a term paper accompanied by properly formatted and reputable bibliographic citations.

The success of the program depends upon the student being able to accomplish the set objectives. Measurement and evaluation of this service has just begun.

Often the librarian plays an important part in refining the definition of the topic, and in a few cases, actually helping the student select the topic. The selection of a term paper topic is not an objective of the service, but in some cases becomes a necessity. Ideally, all students would come to the library with a well-defined topic approved by the instructor. Some topics relate to a wide range of readily accessible literature (such as "Capital Punishment") and others are specialized (such as the "Role of Women in the *Iliad* and the *Odyssey*") or current (like "Star Wars"). The librarian may be presented with the problem of selection or with the problem of locating any information at all. In each case the librarian's role is different. Helping a student select from a mass of material requires wide general knowledge and good judgment -- helping a student locate specialized or current information requires bibliographic expertise. Topics are recorded and this list is then used for the future design of bibliographies, research guides and collection development.

Term paper counseling is a relatively new and innovative branch of library instruction. It offers a good opportunity for personal interaction and guidance. This spring the Undergraduate Library offered 152 hours of counseling, involved twenty-five library faculty and offered help to over 600 students. When polled for their responses both the students and library faculty were highly positive. With faculty and student enthusiasm and good publicity in the classroom and in the media the service flourishes.

Without the visible support of the library administration such programs as these outlined could not continue. The top administrative library faculty have actively participated in the freshman instructional program (this spring the University Librarian and the Director of Technical Services scheduled counseling hours) and their interest serves as an example of priority for other librarians. As publication pressures mount for the library faculty it could be cause for less activity in volunteer instructional programs. Fortunately, the library administration has recently deemed such volunteer participation as "service" and approved it as a part of the scheduled 30 hour work week, outside of the 10 hours allotted for research. Because of such actions our programs are thriving.

Library instruction at the University of Illinois Undergraduate Library is in a formative stage. Four years ago there was no cohesive freshman instructional program; only a walking tour. We have other programs to introduce and perfect. We look forward to changes that the future might bring. New developments in librarianship such as automation will cause a re-definition of what we teach and the methods we use to teach. Still, the basic premise remains: to offer assistance in the use of our resources to the undergraduate students and to educate them bibliographically.

NOTES

1. Glogoff, S.J. and Seeds, R.S. "Interest among Librarians to Participate in Library-Related Instruction at the Pennsylvania State University Libraries," *Pennsylvania Library Association Bulletin*, May, 1976, pp55–56.

2. Hills, P.J. "Library Instruction and the Development of the Individual," *Journal of Librarianship*, 6(4) October, 1974, pp258–259.

LATENT IMAGE TECHNOLOGY FOR FEEDBACK IN LIBRARY INSTRUCTION

John R. Lincoln
Arts and Sciences Library
Lansing Community College

The purpose of this presentation is to describe one of the library instruction programs at Lansing Community College, and the latent image technology which is used to provide instant feedback to the students.

Over 19,000 students attend LCC, and one of the programs offered to students who wish to participate is a College Reading Survival Skills Workshop. This workshop is given just before the beginning of Fall term. It is an intensive one week course in study skills, comprehension improvement, speed reading, and library skills. During the week the student spends 2½ to 3 hours in library instruction. The library instruction consists of a 14 minute sound slide introduction to the library presented in the planetarium (a very media--intensive room), followed by a workbook which provides a hands--on experience with different library tools in the Arts and Sciences Library at LCC.

There are at least two different philosophies of how one should go about teaching. One is to tell the learners what you are going to tell them, then tell them, then tell them what you have told them. Another method is less direct. As Alexander Pope said it, "Men must be taught as if you taught them not. And things unknown proposed as things forgot." The first method is well suited to learning in the cognitive domain. The second, perhaps, is better suited to the affective domain.

Library instruction in this program is a combination of both methods. The affective dimension, the attitudes the students gain toward the library and their attitudes toward their own abilities to function in the library, are at least as important as any specific facts they will learn.

The sound slide program has two purposes. The first is to create an attitude toward the library. The library is presented as a congenial, non--threatening place where students can find the resources they need and can get some help when they want it. The program is designed to break down mental barriers students may possess toward using the library.

Remember, libraries are intimidating places for many people, either because of the atmosphere of the library itself in some cases, ignorance about what the library really is, or just the student's sense of personal insecurity and inadequacy. Sometimes the library must be de--mythologized.

The second purpose is cognitive. The students should know about some of the resources available to them in the library. Four resources are identified, along with an evaluation of what each resource is best suited to do and the method of gaining access to that resource. The four resources are: books, periodicals, A--V or non--print materials, and the reference librarians. For many students one of the most important things they will learn in their initial contact with the library is that the librarian can be useful, and may even be on their side.

In addition, three specific tools are presented in more detail because these tools are apt to be unfamiliar to entering students, and unless they have some concept of the functions of these tools, students won't be tempted to use them. These tools are the LC Subject Headings List, Newsbank, and the "Focus on" series. The Focus ons are pathfinders which provide search strategies for finding information on specific subjects in the LCC Library.

The sound slide program introduces some basic concepts that the students would not gain from the workbook alone -- concepts such as the function of the LC Subject Headings List. In the work--book the students actually use the LC Subject Headings List, but without the previous introduction they might not understand why they are using it.

After the introductory program the students go directly to the library where the workbook forces them to get their hands on a variety of library tools.

A basic consideration in the design of the workbook had to do with logistics. The workbook had to be designed so that as many as thirty--six students could be in the library at the same time, have a hands--on experience using selected tools, and not get in each other's way. To accomplish this, we distribute thirty--six different versions of the workbook to each group of students. Actually, there were only six different sets of questions in the workbooks, but there are also six different arrangements of the pages. This yields thirty--six different workbooks.

Each page of the workbook forms a complete unit. One unit is on How to Find a Book by Its Call Number. Other units are Biog--raphies and Names, Quotes and Poetry, Indexes to Parts of Books, How to Find a Book in the Card Catalog, Which Subjects are in the

Card Catalog?, Periodical Indexes, Book Reviews, Encyclopedias, Dictionaries, Almanacs and Statistics. When six students go to the card catalog to find the answers to the questions in their workbooks, they go to six different drawers. At the same time six other students are beginning the periodicals units by looking into six different volumes of the *Readers' Guide*, and so on.

Because each unit is designed to require about the same amount of time to complete, the students are able to move through the booklet from unit to unit without any serious crowding or having to wait to get at a needed tool because other students are already using it. The Library is also fortunate to have multiple copies of some of the tools such as *Bartlett's Familiar Quotations*.

To understand more about the structure of the workbook we need to look at some of its objectives.

The first objective is to provide a positive hands-on experience in using the library. The workbook makes using the library unnaturally easy. It grossly oversimplifies and is designed so that students do not encounter complicated and confusing situations. Using the library is not simple for the uninitiated, and the workbook avoids throwing them any curves. Once the students have some self-confidence in their own abilities, then there will be ample opportunities for them to discover the problems one normally encounters. Meanwhile, the emphasis is on providing a positive experience. To accomplish this, each question must be constructed with great care. If a students will need to look up a term in an index, make certain that that term doesn't lead him to too many different places. For each question, make certain that the student will actually find the terms he could reasonably be expected to look under in an index. For *Bartlett's Familiar Quotations* "Peel me a grape," a quote from Mae West, is ideal because either of the key words the student might look under, "peel" or "grape," has only a few entries in the index. With carefully constructed questions students can readily negotiate the various library tools, and the functions and structures of those tools will appear obvious.

A second objective is how to use an index. One of the basic keys to using a library is knowing how to use indexes. Students who can't use indexes are doomed to endless browsing. Although browsing has its own rewards, it is a very inefficient search strategy.

The library presents an amazing array of types of indexes to students. The workbook confronts students with many variations of the index theme in the hope that they will achieve some sophistication in negotiating indexes. To successfully complete the workbook students must use indexes in many different forms -- author, title, subject, key-word; indexes that are in straight alphabetical order, others that are subdivided; indexes that are cumulative, and others that are chronologically limited such as periodical indexes. Sometimes students must discern the purpose of the index: some indexes are to the contents of the book in which the index appears, others to the contents of a set of books, others to sections within books, and finally the card catalog which is an index to holdings of the entire library. The workbook is an exercise in generalization and discrimination in the use of indexes.

The third objective is to create an awareness of the resources available in the library. Students should have some idea of the potential of the library for them, or they will never venture to use it. The questions in the workbook deal with a variety of types of information and require the students to use a variety of tools to find the answers. In the evaluations many students express surprise at how many different kinds of questions could be answered in the library; they got the message!

One of the important resources that the students learn about while completing the workbook is the reference librarian. At all times there are two reference librarians circulating among the students to give help when asked, or offering help when the students appear to need some guidance. Even the students who never need the assistance of a librarian see enough instances where the librarians are helping others so that they learn that they will be able to approach a librarian when the need arises.

A typical page in the workbook has very little instruction printed on it. Students don't like to read long explanations. The top half of the page generally lists two or three tools with just enough information to provide a prompt for the student to select the appropriate tools for answering the questions which are printed at the bottom of the page. The unit on "Dictionaries" assumes that students already possess some kind of a concept of "dictionary." Therefore, that concept is built on and expanded to include specialized dictionaries of types which the student would not normally even imagine.

The bottom of the page has questions with multiple choice answers. When students have located the desired information *and have interpreted it correctly*, they can make the correct choices. They indicate their choices by filling in the spaces between the parentheses in front of their choices with a latent image developer. The latent image developer looks much like a highlighter pen, the kind that students use to deface their textbooks and to personalize the volumes in a library. As soon as the choices are made with the latent image developer students receive instant feedback as to whether the choices were correct or not. When the choices are correct, words such as "yes," "of course," or "okay" appear and the students have received some positive reinforcement. When the choices are incorrect, students are encouraged to "try again." Before looking at the technology that makes this instant feedback possible, let's look at the importance of feedback itself. Early research by Ross, and more recently by others, indicates that delaying the knowledge of results decreases the amount of learning. In other words, the longer the delay in providing feedback to the student, the lower the rate of learning. This research is discussed in Godwin C. Chu and Wilbur Schramm, *Learning from Television: What the Research Says*; ERIC Document No. ED014900, pp94--97.

With the instant feedback provided by the workbook, students know immediately whether or not they have performed successfully. If they have not performed successfully, then they can try again because they still have the tools they are working with in their hands.

Instant feedback increases learning, but it has had another effect that was not anticipated. The previous year we had used essentially the same workbook except that the answers were recorded on a machine scorable card. Students did not know until the completion of the workbook which questions they had answered correctly. Many students became discouraged. They either did not complete the score card at all, or at some point they began to randomly select answers. Approximately 20–25% of the students failed to complete the workbook: they simply gave up. The next year using essentially the same workbook except that this time it was in a format to provide instant feedback, fewer than 5% of the students gave up. Instant feedback provides the positive reinforcement students need to complete the workbook. This undoubtedly influences their feelings about the workbook assignment, and thus their feelings about the library itself.

Students are not the only ones who benefit from instant feedback. The librarians are better able to observe the students' progress. By looking over shoulders and noticing what kinds of feedback different students are receiving, the librarians are able to offer guidance to those students who need it. In the process we are able to discover what those students are doing wrong and what they do not understand. As a result of this feedback to the librarians, some of the units in the workbook are undergoing extensive revision.

The technology used in the workbook to achieve the instant feedback is quite simple: it is basically making a spirit master, or ditto. Just type the text material you want onto a spirit master leaving blank spaces where you want invisible responses to appear. Then, remove the spirit carbon and insert in its place a latent image transfer sheet produced by the A.B. Dick Company. Then, type or draw in the invisible responses. When the spirit master is run on the duplicating machine, both the visible and the invisible information is printed simultaneously. When the students use the materials, their latent image developers interact chemically to make the latent images appear.

For the workbook at LCC we wanted a better quality of printing than is produced by a spirit master, so we had the visible text printed commercially, then reprinted each page on a spirit master duplicating machine to put on the latent image. We encountered some difficulties in keeping the two images in register. Since what the spirit master was printing was invisible, we couldn't tell if it was printing it in the right place. Actually, this is only a minor problem and is easily overcome by printing some visible guidemarks on the spirit master. These visible guidemarks help you to keep the visible and invisible printing in register. This is only a problem when the first printing is done separately and you must later reprint for the latent image. Normally everything is done in one step with the spirit duplicating machine.

Latent image technology is simple to utilize, even on the smallest scale, and the feedback it provides to students and to librarians is invaluable. How it can be utilized in your library instruction program is limited only by your ingenuity.

LIBRARY INSTRUCTION WITH SLIDES AND SLIDE/TAPES

Judith L. Violette
Head, Reference Department
Indiana University–Purdue University at Fort Wayne

I want to share with you today some of the factors which led to our use of slides for library instruction, as well as some general advantages and disadvantages of the medium. In doing this, I will be using several examples from our slide programs.

Indiana University–Purdue University at Fort Wayne is a commuter campus in northeastern Indiana. Although it is a regional campus for both Indiana University and for Purdue University, it is semi–autonomous and has a single academic administration reporting to the two respective presidents. Being the stepchild of two arch–rival institutions has caused some identity problems for us, but both "parents" agree that we should remain a "branch" campus. Otherwise the mission of our campus is defined by the Indiana Commission on Higher Education which calls for us to establish programs that meet the needs of local citizens. This mission gives the campus a community college atmosphere although there are fully 90 degree programs available, including twelve master's programs.

A library instruction program has been in existence for nearly the entire 14 years the joint campus has existed. It has evolved from guided tours and "on demand" bibliographic lectures to a more organized program based on planned objectives and goals. Lately we have at least started, and in some cases, completed, organizational tasks we should have performed years ago. We are grateful for the ACRL Guidelines for Bibliographic Instruction in Academic Libraries (1) for suggesting what tasks should be performed to establish a well–organized program.

Our program reflects the nature of the campus, its curricula, its student body and the relatively small size of our library staff. Your program should reflect the nature of your campus in relation to your library resources.

While I do not wish to bore you with our institutional data, the statistics I am about to share with you are the central reasons for the course our program is taking and will, perhaps, serve as an example of factors to consider in your own self--study.

With an average age of 25.1, our student body is, in general, older and more mature than those found on some campuses. They are serious students and they have no time to waste.

CHARACTERISTICS OF THE STUDENT BODY
42% are married
32% have children
25.1 is the average age
16–76 is the age range

Not only do family responsibilities conflict with their study time, but a great many have job conflicts as well. In fact, half of our students are enrolled less than full time. So although there are around 9,000 potential library users on campus each semester, the full time equivalency is only around 5,000.

EMPLOYMENT
78% of the students are employed
55% employed over half time
38% employed 40 hours or more

All of our students commute. And many commute from great distances.

COMMUTING
100% commute
71.3% from Allen County
75% of the student body commutes an
average distance of 6 miles or more one
way

Is it hard to believe that in a survey (2) taken recently, 41% of the respondents admitted spending essentially no time on campus outside of classes?

Taking these and other factors in consideration, we know that the library instruction program we are developing has to meet the needs of an elusive group of students who already have countless demands on their time and energy. We know that our program must be flexible and it must be as individualized as possible, providing plenty of opportunity for independent study.

We have adopted overall objectives that are probably fairly universal: We would like for our students to be familiar with our library services, facilities and resources. We would like for our students to achieve independence and competence in understanding and utilizing certain specific library resources. We would like for our students to be able to develop sound search strategies for finding and integrating information from a wide variety of library resources. And we would like for our students to develop a positive attitude toward the library which will promote life--long library use.

To achieve these objectives in a program that is based on independent learning, we have been developing a series of learning packages, each of which consists of a printed guide, a slide or slide/tape program and a workbook--type exercise. We have let necessity dictate our priorities in producing these. Some units are integrated into the freshman English composition curriculum. We have developed some units for our term paper clinic in response to a repeated need. Our program on *Psychological Abstracts* was produced one semester after two hundred students arrived on the same day to learn how to use it. They came unannounced, sent by a new professor! We conferred with him and were at least ready for his classes the following semester.

There are several advantages to slides and slide/tapes which have contributed to our selection of them as the primary audio--visual medium in our library.

First, they fit easily into several aspects of our library instruction program. Our program exists on three levels: orientation, basic skills and course–related instruction. We use slides in all of these areas as well as in our promotional materials.

We can -- and do -- use slides alone in a classroom and then in combination with a tape for "on demand" individualized instruction. In some cases rather than add a tape, we add a few extra captioned slides, such as a lead–in to a *New York Times* entry. Having these units on hand helps save librarians time in repeating the same instruction over and over.

Slides and slide/tape programs are easy to update. Due to the changing nature of libraries and of library resources this aspect is essential for library instructional materials. If the index changes titles, you just exchange one slide for a new one. Constant monitoring of slide programs for possible revisions is in fact an absolute requirement.

With slides, we can be assured that the students in different classes receive the same core information for each unit and that we remember to cover everything we have deemed essential in our objectives. Especially for librarians new to teaching, well–planned slides can be excellent prompters. And they act as outline guides for students as well. Although each program may have the same core information, with additional slides we can tailor the unit to a specific class project or assignment.

Given the nature of most library instruction situations, the ability to show enlargements of catalog cards and other index entries is certainly one of the most important advantages of using slides.

Another advantage of slides over other media is that we can control both sequence and timing. And when a well--written script is put on tape, the sequence and timing become even more of a factor. Also, by using slides or slide/tapes, we are forced to set our objectives carefully and to prepare our presentation in advance. A series of slides taken from our *MLA Bibliography* program illus--trate the effect of sequential overlays usually associated with over--head transparencies which can also be accomplished with slides.

Film and video recording are media generally used to show motion. But even motion can be indicated by a series of slides. This kind of series sequence for finding periodicals appears in several of our programs.

Slides are versatile in themselves. They can be photographic or graphic or a combination of the two. They can show panoramas or close--ups. And you need not be a graphic artist to make camera-ready copy for slides. There are thousands of free and inexpensive picture sources in a library, among them, annual reports, advertise-ments, brochures, catalogs and periodicals. Using a primary type-writer and construction paper, you can make very inexpensive and very effective slide material. In some slides, we have hollowed out an advertisement and filled the space with our own propaganda. One message was reproduced from gift wrap paper! And what would we do without our favorite cartoons! Excellent slide material is often provided by publishers themselves as in an *American Statistics Index* entry or in an explanation of the *Essay and General Literature Index*. For our Term Paper Clinic promotional slides, we borrowed from a film catalog.

And slides present an impact rarely achieved by words alone. An examination of the educational literature reveals several studies on the reinforcement value of visual material interplayed with audio. We try to achieve additional emphasis by repeating examples from our guides in our slide programs.

But using slides is not all advantageous. Larry Hardesty, in his survey (3) of the use of slide/tape presentations in academic li-braries, uncovered several problems for librarians.

One problem is certainly cost, both in terms of money and in terms of time. Unfortunately, we cannot determine the cost of our productions because much of the graphic and all of the photographic work is provided for us with no charge and with no cost accounting. We know, however, that it takes approximately forty hours of a librarian's time to prepare one 20--minute program. Add to this the cost of equipment and the cost of the photography and the package becomes even more expensive.

Evaluation techniques and in general the lack of any evaluation of slide materials is a major problem of the medium.

There are very few slide productions available to academic librarians. This situation is changing, but we need to establish more library instruction materials directories and clearinghouses similar to LOEX across the country. Maybe we need to form cooperative agreements between specific libraries for the preparation of slide programs in order to build up a library of slide programs available locally and in order to reduce the duplication of efforts currently in evidence. Most libraries would probably want to adapt a commercial program or even another library's program to their own situation, so time and expense would still be a factor.

A new problem is copyright. How long before the Wilson Company starts to sue us for making slides of *Readers' Guide* entries? How long before the *New York Times* demands royalties for money gained in selling slides of their materials? Writing for copyright clearance takes a great deal of time.

Not wishing to end on such a negative note, I hope you will be inspired to at least *try* slides. They certainly add interest to what can be very drab and colorless library instructional materials.

REFERENCES

1. "Toward Guidelines for Bibliographic Instruction in Academic Libraries." *College & Research Libraries News*, No. 5 (May, 1975): pp137–139; pp169–171.

2. "Student Life/Program Report at Indiana University–Purdue University at Fort Wayne." December 23, 1977.

3. Hardesty, Larry. "Use of Slide–Tape Presentations in Academic Libraries: A State–of–the–Art Survey." *Journal of Academic Librarianship*, 3 (July, 1977): pp137–140. (Summary of ERIC Document, ED 116711.)

LIBRARY INSTRUCTION: SOME OBSERVATIONS FROM THE PAST AND SOME QUESTIONS FOR THE FUTURE

Edward G. Holley, Dean
School of Library Science
The University of North Carolina
Chapel Hill

Seven years have now passed since the first Library Orientation Conference was held at Eastern Michigan University in 1971. Not quite a decade, and therefore a relatively short period of time in human history, but those years have been a time of turmoil for the library profession, of stabilized budgets in higher education, and of severe inflationary pressures upon academic libraries. All of us are aware that, in terms dear to the hearts of management experts, the next decade is likely to be a period when directors of libraries must be concerned with "the management of decline," though whether that decline will be quite as severe as some have envisioned is not yet clear.

What has happened during that decade to the cause of library orientation, or bibliographic instruction, or user education, or bibliographic education, or library instruction (whatever term you choose to call it), to which some of you have devoted so much time and energy?

As an individual somewhat outside the mainstream of the movement itself, I believe that there have been three major influences on library service operations in the last decade which are worth noting.

The first of these was the Library–College idea, a program I would designate as representing the sentimental school of library service. For its devotees, chanting the litany, "When a college is a library and a library is a college, it is a Library–College," the Library–College was an idea whose time had come. Although it has not influenced significantly the largest academic libraries and has been subjected to some rather strong criticism, it appears to me to have launched us into this era of renewed efforts at relating the library to the instructional program. The literature on the Library–College idea is extensive and there is no point in rehearsing for this audience its main contribution in calling attention to the need to promote learning through personalized study by using the library, quite literally, as the heart of the instructional process. A couple of issues of the Drexel *Library Quarterly* (1968), books and articles by its high priests, Louis Shores, Robert T. Jordan, Howard Clayton, and others, and two current serials, *Omnibus* and *Learning Today*, are ample evidence of the struggle to give the library a larger role in the groves of academe. From the publications of the Library--College movement, we might suspect that it is a prosperous and hearty group, but when one examines the names of the individuals associated with the publications, they seem to be the same ones who have been involved from the beginning. While still flourishing in some places, the Library--College idea may well be dying of old age at thirty, as critic Fay Blake has claimed. (*Wilson Library Bulletin*, January, 1970.)

The second program, beginning in 1969 and continuing in a slightly enlarged format today, was the College Library Program, a joint project of the Council on Library Resources and the National Endowment for the Humanities. As most of you are aware, this program made grants of $50,000 over a five--year period to about two dozen colleges and universities to see if they could develop innovative methods of relating the library to the educational programs of the institutions. A number of those projects have now been completed and, in the summer of 1975, it was my privilege to visit eight of them and examine what had actually been accomplished.

Let me just share with you some of my observations on the College Library Program: 1) you often cannot tell from a description of a project or its annual reports what is actually happening at an institution because most librarians don't write very well; 2) significant programs are often successful in the most unexpected of institutions; 3) some institutions used these funds for fairly pedestrian projects which had little results; and 4) the programs from which one can sometimes learn the most are those that have failed, but you'll rarely hear about them because most of us are more interested in writing up our successes than we are our failures. On that last point, let me add that librarians are no different from anyone else in higher education; despite our lip--service to the significance of negative results, we don't really believe it.

Some day someone ought to write up the failure of Hampshire College as an experimental college which started with one set of psychological assumptions, and found that they were wrong and had to change both library and institution to accommodate another set of assumptions. Essentially the college was planned to emphasize living and learning, with much of the instruction designed to be non--print oriented and take place in the dormitories. One of the interesting discoveries was that students don't like living and learning together, faculty who are trained in traditional universities are not likely to abandon their print--oriented teaching, and independent study makes heavier demand on print materials than was ever anticipated. Thus a stronger print library became necessary and created other problems in serving users well.

One of the most innovative programs I saw on my summer, 1975 visits was the one in which my colleague, Fred Roper, is involved at Hampden-Sydney College, a small liberal arts college for men in Virginia. Each summer Dr. Roper conducts a one-week "Library Refresher Course" for ten to fifteen members of the faculty. The course is designed to provide the faculty with an overview of reference books and bibliographies which can be used to strengthen their independent study courses and also to enable them to produce a literature guide for their own subject area. As might be imagined, several faculty initially expressed skepticism at being taught by a mere "library science faculty member" and signed up solely for the $200 honorarium. To their great surprise, most of them discovered they learned much from the course. By the end of the five-year period most of the Hampden Sydney faculty will have had a chance to take the course. Despite their high praise for the teacher and the course, I wondered aloud if this approach might work in a larger institution and some thought it probably wouldn't. University faculty don't take kindly to the idea that they may not know the literature of their field or that they might learn something from someone whose expertise is the information base in a subject area. But Dr. Roper's mini-reference course, allied with the vigorous efforts of a new Reference-Coordinator during the regular nine months, has obviously opened up new vistas for the Hampden-Sydney faculty in terms of resources available for instruction. Lest you think I skewed the results, I want to add that I met with several groups of faculty to discuss the program and insisted that librarians not be present.

A.P. Marshall has earlier mentioned other institutions in this College Library Program and so I will merely note that two historically Negro colleges, Dillard and Jackson State, seemed to me to be doing a good job in integrating the library with new curricular developments, and the University of Richmond has demonstrated what can be done to improve course upgrading by funding released time for certain faculty members. Eastern Michigan's data was presented in considerable detail at this conference a year or two ago, so I will comment only that it is one of the most thoroughly documented programs I have seen. The other projects I visited seemed to me to have fairly traditional approaches to library instruction. Let me add that for the modest amount of money expended, even with a few failures, the College Library Program has had a major impact in focusing attention on our service approach to users.

The important point to be made here is that the College Library Program, about which one can find little in the published literature of librarianship, has been an important influence on the evolution of bibliographic education during this decade. Its major weakness, from my point of view, is that most of the grants have been awarded to small liberal arts colleges where success is virtually assured. For if one cannot develop a successful library program to a relatively homogeneous college of 1,000--1,500 students and a faculty of 50 to 100, there seems little hope at all for larger institutions with so many diverse constituencies to be served. Alas, the institutions most needing bibliographic education are probably the large research universities with ten, or twenty, or thirty thousand students, and the evidence of experimental projects or new approaches to user education in such institutions is minimal. Granted that the University of California at Berkeley has long had a formal course which appears quite popular with undergraduates and that a few other large institutions have adapted some elements of multi-media approaches developed at smaller institutions, I still think my observation, or criticism if you like, is valid. Up to this point the largest and most complex universities have not been *directly* affected by the College Library Program.

The third major influence seems to me to be Eastern Michigan University's annual Library Orientation Conferences, which have brought together numerous individuals interested in exchanging ideas and learning new methods of achieving the bibliographic education task effectively. Allied with the conference is Project LOEX, which collects data to share with those who may be contemplating new programs. I must insert here a comment made by one of my North Carolina colleagues who urged me to tell you that bibliographic instruction librarians should be advised to read the literature before they start ambitious bibliographic programs. Her impression is that we continue to repeat each other's mistakes because we do not read the literature *first*. That seems a particularly appalling thing to say about librarians who are noted for mining the literature for other people. Despite Project LOEX, however, there are still librarians who launch into major instructional projects with little knowledge of what has already been tried and, perhaps, found wanting. Nonetheless, the EMU conferences, with their published proceedings, have undoubtedly influenced the library instruction movement, because this has been the one place where the topic of bibliographic education could find a focus once a year. As most of you are aware, only recently has the American Library Association formed a Library Instruction Round Table and the Association of College and Research Libraries issued its "Guidelines for

Bibliographic Instruction in Academic Libraries" only in April, 1977. So this conference and its allied data base have been important in at least raising the consciousness of academic librarians about bibliographic education.

Now all three major influences, which I have isolated as significant, take as their basis a concept recently expressed to me by the dean of a liberal arts college in North Carolina who is looking for a new chief librarian. Said she, "What I really would like to have is a librarian who can relate our library to the educational program. Is that a dream, or dare I hope that I can find someone like that?" I assured her that she was not dreaming, and that there had never been a time when more capable librarians were interested in and prepared to work vigorously to make the library more effective in the educational process. For it does seem clear to some of us that the survival of the library in higher education, or even, as I suggested in the Jerrold Orne Festschrift *Academic Libraries by the Year 2000* (1977), the survival of the liberal arts college itself, may very well depend upon how well we make the library an integral part of the educational program. Viewed in those terms, cutting the library budget may very well be the most expensive mistake any institution makes, for you could eliminate the entire library budget in most colleges and not save more than $75–100,000 per year. Moreover, for the small college, a strong bibliographic education program may be one of the unique selling points as it competes for students with the larger institutions.

But I am getting ahead of myself. Let us confess that bibliographic education did not spring full blown from the head of Louis Shores in the early thirties and find itself reborn in the sixties. There has been an ebb and flow of library instruction in librarianship over the more than one hundred years of its existence as an organized profession in this country. John Edmands and William Frederick Poole at Yale produced what came to be known as *Poole's Index*, chiefly to help students make effective use of a literary society library. The much-maligned John Langdon Sibley opened up the library at Harvard in the eighteen-fifties, a process that was continued by his successor Justin Winsor. Otis Hall Robinson at the University of Rochester noted that he felt himself a failure when students graduated from the University without knowing how to use the library. If you would learn how often history repeats itself, read again the October, 1877, *Library Journal*, which is devoted to college libraries and their use. (See also my "Academic Libraries in 1876," *College and Research Libraries*, January, 1976.)

Periodically since then academic libraries have stressed library use, a necessity when the German seminar method was introduced into American universities in the late nineteenth century, stimulated by the emerging land-grant universities, encouraged by the Columbia and Swarthmore general education programs, and stymied by the burgeoning enrollments in post-World War II America. B. Lamar Johnson's *Vitalizing a College Library* in 1939 showed how easy it was to make a virtue out of necessity and the "reluctant librarian" B. Harvie Branscomb called attention to how little use colleges made of one of their most expensive resources in his landmark work, *Teaching with Books*. Significantly, both books appeared at a time of financial distress for higher education when boards and administrators were taking a hard look at all cost elements.

Like other academicians, however, librarians respond to the needs of the time. Fraternity and dormitory librarians have been tried time and again in higher education, usually with modest results. Changes in the curriculum have often led to new approaches to library service as indeed they should. No librarian can ignore the impact which the current attempts at reform of the undergraduate program at Harvard are likely to have on all universities in the decade of the eighties. The Carnegie Foundation for the Advancement of Teaching has recently called the liberal arts a disaster area in higher education and the new look at the undergraduate curriculum will doubtless move back toward more structure and less relaxed standards. Whether this more conservative approach will have the same kind of impact the laissez-faire *General Education in a Free Society* had in the late forties, we don't yet know. The post-World War II expansion saw chief attention to stronger collections and larger buildings to house them, but as early as 1958 the late Donald Coney wrote an article wondering about how we would handle the hordes of students who would soon be clamoring, "Where did you go? To the library. What did you get? Nothing." (*College and Research Libraries*, May, 1958.) The undergraduate library was built on many large campuses, partly to serve better the undergraduate students, and partly to get them out of the research libraries where they were bothering the faculty and graduate students. The ultimate heresy in any large institution may well be the view that the disproportionate number of undergraduate students deserve at least as good library service as do the faculty, graduate and professional students.

Fundamental to any consideration of bibliographic education, or curriculum reform, is the question "Are the students being educated well?" The faculty thought this was the major question for student unrest in the sixties, though as Stadtman and Riesman indicated in their book, *Academic Transformation*, that was not really the major student concern. It was a faculty concern. And neither that overworked word "relevance," nor ethnic studies, nor experimental colleges did much to solve persistent problems. Perhaps that's because major problems rarely *are* solved. We either learn to live with them or make modest accommodations to meet current pressures.

Where are we now? There seems to be a genuine interest on the part of faculty and librarians to look more closely at what they are doing and to want answers to the question, "Are students learning what they need to know?" I pose that question not in any narrow vocational sense, but in the larger sense of what it takes to make a student an educated person. The recent articles by Richard de Gennaro and others have asked us to look again at how we are allocating library resources. Do we really need to focus our attention as much on collection building as we do on service to users? Academic librarians, with their prejudices in favor of the large central library filled with unique titles, might well take a look at their brothers and sisters in the special libraries who have managed to target resources from a relatively small collection, with adequate back--up elsewhere, to serve the intensive use of a specialized clientele. Although I am well aware of the competing needs and vastly different programs of most university libraries as opposed to the special libraries' more narrow programs, I think the comparison is still worth making. It seems unlikely that most students and/or faculty need vast quantities of the world's literature to serve their specific needs. The master's student in library science may well be better served by two copies of *American Libraries* than by one copy of *American Libraries* and a subscription to the *Singapore Journal of Library Science*.

What falls out, of course, is that special and academic libraries are labor--intensive operations and that library resources and services are costly any way you look at the problem. Bibliographic education ultimately has to face the same problem other library operations face: limited human and financial resources. In most cases bibliographic education will not receive large additional increases in funds but will have to battle for a larger proportion of stabilized library budgets. Our formula--based society is unlikely to adopt the Library--College concept of every faculty member a librarian and vice versa. Eventually we all have to become concerned with the fact that we may be victims of our own success. Can we, without stifling initiative, create modest programs of bibliographic instruction at a basic level and provide some specialized information service for those who need it, i.e., graduate and professional students and faculty? There are likely to be only so many librarians for any given number of students, just as there has traditionally been a ratio of one faculty member for 15--17 undergraduate students and one for 10–12 graduate students. However much we might wish otherwise, it is apparent that large additional resources are not likely to be provided and that there is potentially a limited number of positions which can be recaptured from better bibliographic control or declining numbers of staff in technical services, or more carefully targeted book funds. Alternatives in library budgeting are possible, even necessary, but they are limited. A consideration we dare not avoid is that success in any library service program has both staff and collection consequences. Almost assuredly a successful bibliographic education program will lay the groundwork for future heavy staff workloads and increased demands for more print and non-print materials. For that reason, those involved in this process have concentrated, correctly in my opinion, in creating better organizations and using non--personal resources to help students help themselves. Like all other operations library instruction must be organized for maximum efficiency. There will be a need for even better approaches to this financial problem in the future.

In closing let me raise a few questions for further consideration. In order to target our financial and human resources to accomplish the library service task, all academic librarians would be well advised to ask themselves these questions:

1. What *is* the role of the library in the educational process?
2. How have librarians attempted to cope with this role?
3. What is likely to be the future pattern or patterns of attempts to serve users in academic libraries?
4. In the trade--offs so necessary in academe, what is the potential for success?

As you struggle with these questions as they relate to bibliographic education, I wish you well. For basically I do agree with that hundred--year--old dictum of Justin Winsor,

> A collection of good books, with a soul to it in the shape of a good librarian, becomes a vitalized power among the impulses by which the world goes on to improvement. (*LJ* 3:5)

Note: I acknowledge my indebtedness to Dr. Richard Werking, University of Mississippi, Dr. Rose Simon, Guilford College, and my students Beth Kessler and Robert Byrd for their contributions to my thinking on this subject.

EFFECTS OF EVALUATION ON TEACHING METHODS

Mignon Adams
Penfield Library
State University College of New York at Oswego

The emphasis of this afternoon's session is to be on practical applications of evaluation methods, and I intend to be eminently practical. My remarks will be concerned with the application of some simple evaluation methods to the library instruction program at Oswego, one of the four-year institutions of the New York state system. It is only fair to tell you of my biases: most of my experience has been in the area of instructional design, which uses primarily the "systems approach," and so what I have to say will be within the framework of this approach.

Also, I will confine myself today to our experience with course-related instruction. I also teach a credit course, but the assessment and evaluation of this is exactly the same as in any other academic course. However, course-related instruction is quite different; the librarian is a guest, with limited involvement with students – and little knowledge of them.

Course-related instruction at Oswego began seven or eight years ago. At that time, we thought about what students should know about the library, and a typical class presentation might include library locations; how to read a catalog card; and a bibliography of all the sources students might conceivably use (accompanied by a truckful of books). As we taught more classes, we started systematically having classes respond to an evaluation form. Over and over again, we received the response: too much material was covered. We sat back and put some more thought into what we were doing.

As part of this process, we began to gather information regularly about the students we were teaching, primarily through the use of pretests. We found out some interesting things.

First of all, students (unless it was at the beginning of their first semester at Oswego) knew major locations. They didn't need us to provide this information -- they were getting it pretty well on their own -- so this was an obvious block of information we could leave out.

Next, we found that, overwhelmingly, students could identify parts of a catalog card. We find that, while students may not be able to interpret the fine print, they can identify authors, titles, publishers, publication dates, and call numbers. They can use the catalog card for what it was intended: as an index to the library's holdings by author, title, or subject.

Let me insert here that, while I would hesitate to make a generalization about college students based on our findings, there is not much unique about Oswego's student population. We are no more selective than many public institutions; our students come from rural, urban, and suburban high schools from all over New York. Moreover, students enrolled in our Equal Opportunity Program (who do not meet regular entrance requirements) also can identify parts of catalog cards. We felt, then, that this was more information that did not need to be covered.

Readers' Guide was another tool we often covered that students know about. They know what its function is, they can interpret a citation, and they do in fact often use it. They are not, however, familiar with other indexes nor do they use them.

As a result of the pretesting and evaluation we were doing, our teaching began to change. For example, where we previously whizzed through a truckful of books, we now cover only one or two tools a session. In the psychological research courses in which I customarily teach a two-hour session each semester, I cover only *Psychological Abstracts*, methods of finding review articles, and library services such as interlibrary loan.

We also try to tie sessions exactly to assignments: it might be nice to know about the vertical file, but if students don't need to use it to complete their assignments, they won't remember it. Drawing the line between "nice to know" and "essential" is not always easy, but it makes a big difference in student reception.

Finally, we talk less and students do more. Each of our sessions is planned so that about half the time is spent with students actually involved -- usually completing exercises under our supervision. "Students learn by doing" is an old phrase, but it is as true today as it was when Dewey (the other one) coined it.

Let me review the process that we use. First, we determine the audience: what do they already know, and what do they need to know? We do this by pretesting, enough earlier than the library sessions so that the results can influence our teaching, and by talking to the instructors as to the exact nature of their assignments and what the instructors' expectations may be.

The next step is to determine objectives: just what do we expect students to be able to do after instruction? The process of developing objectives is beyond the scope of this paper, but I would stress that clear and somehow measurable objectives are essential if meaningful evaluation is to occur. Remember -- if you do not know where you are going, you cannot determine if you've arrived.

The final step is to determine the effects of your instruction. The classic procedure in instructional design is to administer a post-test which is identical to the pretest; the difference in scores represents the amount of learning that has taken place. However, there are some problems inherent in course-related library instruction which have caused us to alter our procedures.

The primary problem is a lack of time. Many instructors begrudge the time spent in library instruction; they are not gracious about devoting an hour's worth of class time in both pre- and post-testing for one or two hours of instruction. Another problem is the lack of motivation on the part of the student. Evaluation of course-related library instruction is not a part of the course structure. Students are under no pressure to do well, or even to respond at all. However, this lack of pressure leads also to an advantage: students can be honest. If their response is favorable, it is not because they are hoping for a good grade.

In order to meet these problems, we try to evaluate our presentations in several ways. A very old method is that of observation. Are students paying attention? If your class is meeting in two sessions, do students return for the second one? This method has its dangers, though; you are apt to notice and remember only those students at either end of the spectrum (those full of enthusiasm or full of sleep) and you are unlikely to be able to obtain an accurate picture.

The exercises that students do during our session are another method of evaluation. The exercises are designed so that successful completion of them means that students have met our objectives -- or at least can meet them under the controlled environment of a class setting.

It is important, at this point, to keep the principle of "transfer of learning" firmly in mind. Exercises must be as close as possible to the real experience you want students to be competent in. Otherwise, being able to do the exercise teaches students only how to do the exercise. Our worksheets on indexes, for example, require students to be in the index area, locate an appropriate index, and use the actual index itself -- not a copy of a page, or any other facsimile. Students also deal with their own topics, rather than an artificial one given to them.

We also try to systematically gather information from the students after they have completed the assignment or project for which the instruction was planned. The kinds of information we seek from these reactions are these:

---- Did the class session help them complete their projects? We'd

like to know if the kind of information we gave them was indeed what they needed, and, of course, if it wasn't, either no session was needed, or the session should be revamped.
—— Was new information presented? We want to stop covering materials that students feel they already know. Also, since the classroom teacher administers our reaction forms, and thus will probably read them, this information will be of interest to him/her.
—— Did students have positive feelings about the session? For the sake of the future of libraries and ourselves, let us hope that students feel more positive towards libraries at the end of the session than at the beginning. If they feel more negative, the session should never have happened.
—— Did the students have problems completing their projects? If there were problems, we'd like to know if they were caused by lack of knowledge on the part of the student, or by factors we can't affect through library instruction -- missing materials, for example, or an inadequate collection for a particular topic. This information, of course, may be of interest to other areas of the library.
—— Were our presentation skills adequate? It is certainly important to know if we were audible, or used visible transparencies, or were disorganized. However, if feedback on presentation skills is very important to you, this information should be obtained as soon as possible after the class session.

As a final note on our gathering of student reactions, let me mention rating scales. We do not use them. Rating scales are meaningless unless you have a norm to compare them to. If I were to ask you to rate me today on a scale ranging from 1 (poor) to 5 (excellent), and I received an average rating of 4, what would this mean? If you rated all speakers at this conference, and I could compare my 4 to the score of other speakers, I'd have a better idea, but I still don't have enough information. A standard scale, used nationally, would give me still more information -- but such a scale doesn't exist. We do not, therefore, use rating scales.

The process of evaluation at Oswego has been an evolving one. I would like to say that we started from the beginning, doing everything correctly; I would even more like to say that we systematically evaluate our entire program, pinpointing its strengths and weaknesses, and can be accountable for what students learn about the library during their stay at Oswego, Unfortunately, I can't, nor is this information available about any program I'm aware of. However, even rather simple applications of evaluation methods can yield information -- and unexpected information – which can lead you to alter your teaching methods and materials for the better.

EVALUATING STUDENT KNOWLEDGE OF FACILITIES AT THE UNIVERSITY OF COLORADO, COLORADO SPRINGS

Elizabeth Frick
Head of User Services
Library
University of Colorado
Colorado Springs

The final report on the library use survey conducted in the fall of 1977 at the University of Colorado, Colorado Springs (Lou Ellen Crawford, *Confirmation and Interpretation of Student Attitudes toward the Library at the University of Colorado, Colorado Springs*) states that:
> This study was undertaken for the purpose of discovering attitudes toward products and services of the existing system of the Library on the campus . . . .

Further, the research wanted to discover where students perceived the library to fit in the total pattern of their learning while at the University. As the report states:
> Is there a belief among students (and faculty) that teaching methods should encourage student use of library resources? If there is such a philosophy, and if the library is viewed as an integral part of education, then effort might be made to determine the extent to which teaching methods must go in order to encourage library use. (page 1)

The preliminary survey -- the "before" survey, if you will -- was conducted within the first months of a CLR Library Service Enhancement Program grant awarded to the library for the purpose of coordinating and enriching our instructional program. This preliminary survey is to provide us with baseline data prior to a similar survey which will be run eighteen to twenty-four months after that initial survey to study any changes that develop in student attitudes and knowledge.

This talk today is not intended as a technical report on the survey. Copies of the final report will be available through LOEX or through the Library, University of Colorado, Colorado Springs. Today I will give you an outline of the type of survey it was that we conducted, describe for you the first, broad, statistical profile of our students that we see emerging, and begin to relate that to some of the conclusions that I have arrived at concerning libraries in higher education.

For those of you with statistics on your mind, however, let me tell you briefly who did what to whom and with what. The study was conceived and instigated by the library. The library funded it and it was the library that directed it. The questionnaire was designed and the research conducted by a research associate with our sociology department, a woman with broad experience in conducting such studies. The questionnaire was administered to a sample of 15% of our 4,100 students, and was carefully balanced across the four colleges that make up our campus, and across the eighteen or so hours of the day that the university offers courses. It was administered in the classroom in an effort to reach both users and non--users. The brief, straight--forward questionnaire (17 multiple choice questions) was designed using independent variables such as degree status, frequency of use, etc., and dependent variables such as explanations for use patterns, perceptions of the library and librarians, attitudes toward instruction, etc. These questions are spelled out in the final report. The questionnaire was administered to a number of classes, either at the outset or at the close of the class. It was administered, for the most part, by the liaison librarian for that subject area. The librarian was instructed to give a minimum of direction in order to avoid biasing answers. This particular librarian found that good sessions developed occasionally *after* the questionnaire was completed when spontaneous discussion arose about the purpose or directions of the library.

In the end the results of the survey were found to be statistically valid and many of the results are, I think, applicable to other academic libraries with one proviso. Several speakers today have referred to the older student, the exceptional student, etc. The average entering age of our students is 28--29. Some 70% of them hold other jobs. Furthermore, we are a commuter campus without a single dorm. It will be clear that some of our findings, then, will be influenced by these factors.

In addition to the standard, designed questionnaire, we gave the student some optional open--ended questions, asking what he/she liked most about the library, how it could be improved, what sections of the library had provided most help, what he/she felt about the new building as a study environment and so on. For a grasp of the immediate, personal responses to the library, the open--ended questionnaire, the results of which I will not discuss here today, gave me a great deal of insight into the problems of individual students. The computerized, standardized questionnaire gave me more information about aggregate problems, needs and attitudes.

Obviously, the computerized results are so extensive, that again I refer you to the final report. While I will report just a few of our findings here, I will also be reporting some personal conclusions I have made in viewing those findings.

Some interesting facts and correlations stand out.

Forty--eight to forty--nine percent of our students were defined as "high--users" (arbitrarily set at those who use the library at least once a week). Forty--seven percent would be termed "low--users," while five percent said they never used the library on campus.

It is tempting to speculate on how higher education's current trend to train primarily for the job market rather than for the liberally--educated mind, is affecting library use. And it is interesting to cross tabulate our results comparing frequency of library use in the professional schools (particularly business and engineering) with the School of Letters, Arts and Sciences. The majority of our high--to--medium library users are undergraduates in LAS classes. Business and Engineering undergraduates are low users.

The low and non--users blamed primarily (55%) lack of personal time for their low use pattern, the next most frequent reason offered (and it was way back – 21%) was lack of personal awareness of services, hours, etc. These are interesting figures to one interested in bibliographic instruction since presumably better library skills would at once both improve efficiency of the student's search and thus save time for the student, and increase awareness of the library's services, hours, etc. Only 17% said that the library "doing a better job of meeting my needs" would affect their library use. We need to look at the answers to other questions to try to get at what they meant by this. An equal number (18%) felt that if faculty members encouraged library use and/or assigned projects requiring library research, it would affect their use. This is a significant statistic when we learn later that 18% of our student sample have never been given what they would term a research--type assignment. It is also significant that 18% said that increased encouragement to use the library by faculty members would help them use the library more often, when only 3.7% felt that a more helpful library staff would increase their use. Our researcher notes that "Helpful guidance from professors . . . may have had an impact on students' frequency of library use since higher users reported more frequently than lower users that professors' guidance was helpful."

Our students, not surprisingly, knew and used the reserve material, and knew and used the aid--in--finding--information function of the library more than any other aspects.

What did they feel they needed more information about? Slightly more than one--half of the sample said they would like more information about library services. Above all they wanted more information on the periodicals, indexes, and abstracts and on audio-visual material (24% and 23% respectively). Only 8% felt they needed more information about the card catalog! Richard Burton has said:

> He who knows not and knows now he knows not, he is a fool – shun him . . . .

We have no intention of shunning those who know not the catalog, nor know not that they know not. We will confront them. Perhaps an old Italian proverb is more applicable here – "He who knows should rule, and he who does not know should obey."

The librarians at UCCS are still seen primarily as question answerers (65%), secondarily (43%) as book custodians. Only in third place, and a good way behind (12%), were the librarians seen as teachers. We even got one write-in vote as baby-sitters!

However, students are not inflexible and seem to leave room for the librarian to become a teacher as a majority, in fact 59%, of our sample expressed interest in taking library-use classes for credit.

We did not try to test our students on their knowledge of titles or of how to use certain bibliographic resources. We asked only about knowledge and use of resources such as inter-library loan, periodicals on microfilm, the children's literature collection, study hall facilities, gallery, etc. I say this to emphasize first of all that the survey is not designed as a testing of the *educational* value of bibliographic instruction (a test that the profession desperately needs), but a measurement of the degree of knowledge of facilities and services, as well as of attitudes towards those facilities and services, what our researcher calls "personal and attitudinal characteristics." I also point out this emphasis on service knowledge rather than bibliographic knowledge because even at this level we found that the majority of our students had what we had defined as a low degree of knowledge of the library. I hope we shall find that changed when we re-administer this test months from now. At least I trust we shall find the degree of knowledge changed among *advanced* students, though I suspect that attitudes are often set early in life through the public libraries.

What aspect of the library did students perceive as most important to them? Only 18% considered the library *primarily* as a place to study. I view this figure, unlike some of the others, as not necessarily representative of students in other libraries, given the commuter nature of our campus. If I had to guess, I would guess that our student use of other libraries (which we measured) would also be higher than the national average because of this same factor. Thirty-seven percent of our sample listed the fact that the library "provides books" as of first importance to them. But in a breakdown by high-use/low-use, the second most important use to high-users was as a study area, while to low-users it was that the library offers aid in finding information. Both types of users ranked "teaches how to do research" as fifth or last.

In cross-tabulating some of the variables we discovered that our juniors had the greatest percentage of high--users among their ranks, and they showed a high knowledge of the library -- ranking a close third in knowledge to the graduate and seniors. They also rank high, along with freshmen, in their desire for a credit class in library use.

Depending on your viewpoint, it may or may not be surprising that more high--users than low--users want a credit class in library use. At which point, it is appropriate to quote the second line of that same Richard Burton piece that I mentioned earlier:

He who knows not and knows not he knows not, he is a fool -- shun him;

He who knows not and knows he knows not, he is simple – teach him . . . .

There is so much that we would like to have asked. Maybe given unlimited time and an infinitely docile sample, we should have asked more. But this was a modest effort, with relatively modest, but concrete aims. There were certainly some broader conclusions that I drew from this survey.

I sensed in the institutions in which I have worked, and in many of the institutions I have visited, that there is an increasing restlessness in higher education about the lack of communication among the disciplines. The academic library can offer a forum for interaction among the widely separate groups. This integrating aspect of the library needs not just to be said, but to be illustrated on a number of levels. The forum can operate in many ways: through the library program (e.g., lecture series, management of the approval plan, discussion groups, and so on), physical location of the library on campus, architecture and design of the building, skills of the librarians, etc. I believe that not only might the library be viewed, as our report states, "as an integral part of education," but also as performing an integrating function on the campus and in education. The interrelatedness of all knowledge is a lesson that the librarians can teach through the teaching of literature patterns, their similarities and differences. This is one of the ways in which the library is at the heart of the university. My sense, undocumented, is that faculty deep down, know this. I hope it is not stretching our survey to say that the results indicate that students feel the faculty is not acting on that knowledge. My sense, again undocumented, is that students do not know the part the library can play in their education. Certainly this survey did nothing to give the lie to my feeling that while students may come to college with an affection for the library -- and too many of them come without even that – only the best come with any real knowledge of the place it holds in their learning, or of the potential it offers them for a continuing education, for what one writer has called an open--ended education, for making them what another calls "independent learners." This is something they need to learn. I am convinced that this is the most valuable, lasting gift that library instruction can offer students. One of the basic goals of the instructional program at Colorado Springs is to project an image of the library different from the image many students come with.

Further, I am convinced that only in a library aware of its wider, integrating mission, only in such a library is bibliographic instruction offered in an environment appropriate or hospitable to its real message. That is the kind of library we hope to build at the University of Colorado, Colorado Springs.

EVALUATION AS A TOOL FOR PROGRAM DEVELOPMENT

Peter P. Olevnik
Head of Reference
Drake Memorial Library
State University of New York College at Brockport
Brockport, New York

Introduction

How do you provide a meaningful library educational experience for two--hundred students, on a regular basis, without the aid of special funding or additional staff? The answer to this question pro-- vided the basis upon which a program of instruction and orientation was developed for presentation at the library of the State University of New York College at Brockport.

In my talk this afternoon, I will first describe the instruction- orientation program that I and my staff developed. I will discuss the evaluation procedure that we designed, and present, briefly, some of our findings.

The program that we developed is presented in three phases to students enrolled in sections of an English composition course. It has been offered each fall and spring semester since March 1975.

Phase I

The first phase of the program consists of a self--guided taped library tour. To take the tour, students report to the library's Special Materials Center where a portable tape player and headset are checked out to them. They listen to taped commentary as they walk along a pre--arranged route of fifteen stops. The tour covers only those areas of immediate concern and interest to the students, and it takes about twenty--five minutes to complete.

The tour is offered on an individual basis during all hours that the library is open, or it can be made available to an entire class of up to twenty--eight students during a regularly scheduled class period.

Phase II

The second phase in the program consists of a slide/sound presentation which provides instruction in the use of the card catalog, the *Readers' Guide*, the *New York Times Index*, and includes information relating to locating periodicals in the library. For this presentation, students again report to the library's Special Materials Center where they receive instruction by means of Singer Caramate slide-sound players. Because of the small screen size, the players are available for use on an individual basis or to no more than three or four students at one session, during all hours that the library is open. This presentation also lasts about twenty-five minutes.

Phase III

Using knowledge and experience gained in the first two exercises, students are required to complete a thirteen-page workbook designed to a) introduce them to a basic search strategy, and b) to provide a guide to source materials that will be used by them in the completion of a brief biographical paper.

The workbook consists of six exercises arranged by type of reference source or topic: included are biographical dictionaries, encyclopedias, the card catalog, periodical indexes and abstracts, bibliographies, and microforms. For three of the exercise units, students choose one source from an annotated listing of reference sources. The object is for the students to select one work that would include information about the subject of their biographical paper. The remaining three exercise units provide hands-on experiences in using the card catalog, microforms, and bibliographies.

This exercise is presented to an entire class, during a scheduled class period. A librarian provides a brief introduction and works with the students in the completion of the workbook.

Evaluation

The evaluation procedure, planned as an integral part of the three-phase program, provides valuable information for making program revisions; it serves as a gauge of whether the stated objectives are being met; and finally it measures the degree of learning that has taken place.

Pretests and Post-tests

Prior to the presentation of the program, students are tested to determine the level of their library knowledge and skills. A similar test is given several weeks after the program's conclusion to measure their progress or lack of it. Both tests consist of twenty--four, multiple--choice questions that relate directly to the information and instruction presented in the three--phase program.

The tests are scored by computer at the college's Education Communications Center. They provide an overall mean--average score for both the pretest and the post--test, the average pretest and post--test score for each of the program's three phases, and the number and percent of students who answer each question correctly or incorrectly.

Questionnaires

An indispensable aid in helping us re--design and revise the program was the data obtained from questionnaires. One was designed for each phase of the program.

The questionnaires are brief, consisting of six questions each. To give you some idea of the composition of the questionnaire, the first set of questions asks students to indicate, on a scale from one to five, what they thought about such features as usefulness, clarity, and complexity or simplicity in presentation. Two other questions are more open--ended, asking students to offer suggestions to improve the program or describe areas where additional information might be needed.

Regarding the last question about additional information, in the planning stage we had the suggestions tabulated and ranked in order of frequency of request. This proved most helpful. For example, we found that a large number of students requested additional information about microforms. This was true for results tabulated from both the first phase and second phase questionnaires. We therefore expanded our coverage in this area.

As was the case with the tests, completed questionnaires were sent to the college's Educational Communication Center for tabulation by computer. One very encouraging finding was the favorable response to the question concerning whether a student would recommend a particular phase of the program to a friend. They could rate it as "yes" without reservation, "yes . . . if" with reservation or "no," not recommended. For the spring 1975 evaluation period, 90.1 percent said they would recommend the first--phase tape--tour without reservation. For the second--phase slide/sound presentation, the figure was 92.5 percent. Although, I might add, only about one--third found the presentation interesting. For the final phase, the workbook exercise, the figure dropped to 76.9 percent who would recommend it with reservation -- still an acceptable figure. It is interesting to note that while this exercise received the lowest score in terms of its recommendation to others, the improvement between pretest and post-test scores was most pronounced. The average shifted from a pretest score of 58 percent to a post-test score of 83.4 percent, for an increase of nearly 26 percentage points.

A more informal evaluation procedure was applied during the formative stages in the program's development. As tests were being designed, or as we were in the process of developing questionnaires and workbooks, students were chosen randomly to read over the material, complete the tasks being asked, make recommendations, and look for professional jargon or areas of possible confusion.

A great deal was learned by actually presenting the program. For example, initially we designed four workbook exercises: one for the Arts, another for the Social Sciences, the Sciences, and the Humanities. We offered students a choice in terms of their career goals, course majors, and interests. We found, however, that this caused considerable difficulty for them because they had not decided on a major, did not know in which broad area their subject fit, or they simply could not or would not make a choice. We therefore rejected this approach, and after consultation with the teaching faculty involved, chose the more general workbook exercise relating to the biographical paper.

We also conducted post-project meetings with the English Department Faculty and graduate student assistants who did the teaching. These meetings were generally productive in that they offered us a chance to discuss student responses as offered in the classroom, the instructor's observations, and problems of mutual concern.

Conclusion

From the results of our data, we feel that the library has been able to provide meaningful, systematic instruction and orientation to much larger numbers of students, than has been possible in the past with minimal direct library involvement.

Secondly, students have shown a positive response to media-assisted instruction, and librarian-student contact, requested by students, and desired by librarians, was maintained by means of the workbook exercise.

I might add that this presentation, with its emphasis on the method of evaluation, is an overview of a more detailed report of our program, published as part of the Educational Resources Information Center (ERIC) documents collection. The report includes results of data gathered, sample copies of instruction sheets, questionnaires, tests, and the workbook. The report number is ED 134 138. Copies of slides and audio-tapes that were developed for the program are available for loan through the Library Orientation–Instruction Exchange (LOEX) Clearinghouse at Eastern Michigan University.

LIBRARY ORIENTATION AND INSTRUCTION — 1977; AN ANNOTATED REVIEW OF THE LITERATURE

Hannelore B. Rader
Coordinator, Education and Psychology Division
Center of Educational Resources
Eastern Michigan University

The following is an annotated bibliography of materials published in 1977 on orienting users to the library and on instructing them in the use of reference and other resources. A few entries have a 1976 publication date and are included because information about them was not available in time for the 1976 review. Also some entries are not annotated because the compiler was unable to secure a copy of the information.

Included in this list are publications on user instruction in all types of libraries and for all types of users, from the lower elementary levels to adults. It was found that the library literature includes many citations from foreign countries on library instruction but only references to items in the English language have been included.

Once again it is evident that the interest in and preoccupation with library instruction is growing, as seen by comparing this year's number of entries with last year's; there are 36% more entries. Another interesting and encouraging phenomenon bears pointing out -- 18 (19%) of the citations come from non–library professional journals. Because of the increasingly large number of citations, the list this year is arranged by type of library first and within it alphabetically by author.

ACADEMIC LIBRARIES

COMMUNITY AND JUNIOR COLLEGE LIBRARIES

Dale, Doris C. "Mastering Library Research Techniques through Self--Instruction." *Technological Horizons in Education Journal.* 4 (November--December, 1977), pp. 44--46.

Dale, Doris C. "Questions of Concern: Library Services to Community College Students." *Journal of Academic Librarianship.* 3 (May, 1977), pp. 81--84.

The author visited and interviewed 100 librarians in community colleges in six states to assess library service to community college students. Library orientation and instruction was found one of four major services for students and faculty at the surveyed institutions.

Keroack, Ann. *A Basic Behavioral Objectives Library Package.* 1977. 18p. ED 136 819.

Designed for students at N. H. Vocational Technical College, this self--instructional package introduces fresh--men to the use of a small college library. Includes a self--test.

Kinney, Lillie C. "Librarians as Educators." *Community and Junior College Journal.* 47 (May, 1977), pp. 10--11, 27.

Discusses the involvement of the librarians at Onondaga Community College in the teaching--learning process through teaching a one--credit course on the library and by utilizing media for library use instruction. Most importantly, the librarians there employ an open and positive attitude toward users.

Sim, Yong S. *A Self--Guided Library Tour Method at Mercer County Community College. The Learning Theory and Applications Module.* 1976. 37p. ED 135 342.

The self--guided library tour utilizes a cassette tape and a coded floor plan. The document describes the tour and also has appended to it a classroom survey form, a questionnaire for new students and an evaluation form for the tour.

COLLEGE AND UNIVERSITY LIBRARIES

Adams, Roy J. "Teaching Packages for Library User Educa--tion." *Audiovisual Librarian.* 3 (Winter, 1976--77), pp. 100--106.

This article discusses various methods of user education and relates them to specific user needs such as motivation, response, reinforcement and transfer. The author feels that the best user instruction cannot be obtained from a package obtained elsewhere but should be developed at one's own institution.

Biermann, June. "Technological Tools and Toys." *Wilson Library Bulletin.* 52 (September, 1977), p. 26.

A letter commenting on R. Vuturo's article (see below) and advocating less media teaching in library instruction and more live librarian involvement.

Borchuck, Fred P. and Bernice Bergup. *Opportunities and Problems of College Librarians Involved in Classroom Teaching Roles.* 1976. 16p. ED 134 216.
  Describes experiences of 2 college librarians involved in non–library related teaching duties and the effect of this on their professional status.

Bradfield, Valery and others. "Librarians or Academics? User Education at Leicester Polytechnic." *Aslib Proceedings.* 29 (March, 1977), pp. 133–142.
  This article discusses a 2–year experiment in which four academic librarians were engaged in full--time teaching to educate students in the use of resources. Their achievements in relationship to courses in Information Studies is also discussed.

Brand, Marvine. "Using the Chemistry Library: Questions Students Ask." *Journal of College Science Teaching.* 6 (January, 1977), p. 192.
  Outlines briefly how the University of Houston Library deals with chemistry students' orientation to library information.

Breivik, Patricia S. *Open Admissions and the Academic Library.* Chicago: American Library Association, 1977.
  This book deals with the implementation of open admissions in post--secondary education especially in relationship to the academic library. The responsibilities of educators and specifically librarians, in facing the diversity of problems students under open admissions encounter are outlined. The information presented is based on a research project completed by the author at Brooklyn College in 1972. This project dealt with the measurement of the value of library–based instruction in the learning experiences of the educationally disadvantaged.

Breivik, Patricia S. "Resources: The Fourth R." *Community College Frontiers.* 5 (1977), pp. 46--50.

Bristow, Thelma. "Library Learning; the Way to Self–Help in Education." *Education Libraries Bulletin.* Supplement 20 (1970). University of London.

Brooke, Ann and others. *Academic Library Instruction in the Southwest.* 1976. 111p. ED 140 778.
  This is a directory of library instruction programs in 216 academic libraries in the Southwest (Arizona, Arkansas, Louisiana, New Mexico, Oklahoma and Texas). A summary of the information and the survey questionnaire are included.

Carpenter, Eric J. "The Literary Scholar, the Librarian, and the Future of Literary Research." *Literary Research Newsletter.* 2 (October, 1977), pp. 143--155.

This article discusses the reasons why academic librarians, professors and scholars need to cooperate, to further literary research, to improve bibliographic control in the humanities and to provide instruction in library use.

Christensen, T.B. "Information Search in Biochemistry -- A Short Course for Students." *Biochemical Education.* 5 (1977), p. 31.

A Comprehensive Program for User Education for the General Libraries, The University of Texas at Austin. Austin, Texas: University of Texas, 1977.

This document summarizes library user education activities, user needs and program proposals for user education at the University of Texas, Austin. Since 1975 two User Education Committees have been working on formulating a comprehensive user education program for the General Libraries. Questionnaires were utilized to assess needs of users and present status of user education. Goals and objectives were formulated for a 3--stage program.

Culley, James D. and others. "Business Students and the University Library: An Overlooked Element in the Business Curriculum." *Journal of Academic Librarianship.* 2 (January, 1977), pp. 293--296.

This is a study of business students' knowledge and use of library resources based on data collected from graduate and undergraduate students in business courses at the University of Delaware, Wright State University and the University of Maryland. It was found that these students are ill--prepared to use secondary business resources for research and classwork and do not seem to care whether or not this condition is remedied. A few suggestions to improve the situation are given.

Dash, Ursula. "The Self--Guided Library Tour." *Australian Academic and Research Libraries.* 8 (March, 1977), pp. 33--38.

The author discusses the creation of a self--guided library tour at La Trobe University in audio format. Objectives were formulated before the tour was produced. User evaluation of the tour helped improve it.

Evans, A.J. *Education and Training of Users of Scientific and Technical Information.* UNISIST Guide for Teachers. Paris: UNESCO, 1977.

This guide was developed for teachers concerned with developing and conducting information retrieval skills courses, especially in developing countries. This monograph includes information on benefits from user education, planning and preparing courses, course presentation and content, methodology and search techniques, exercises and other hints. Appendixes include tours, handouts, exercises and references.

Fitzgerald, Sylvia. "An Effective Approach to Library Instruction in Departmental Training Courses." *State Librarian.* 25 (1977), p. 25.

Fjallbrant, Nancy. "Evaluation in a User Education Programme." *Journal of Librarianship.* 9 (April, 1977), pp. 83--95.

This is an attempt to outline evaluation in library use instruction by discussing purposes of evaluation, methodology and timing. Also included are a summary of previous attempts of evaluation and the evaluation procedures at Chalmers University of Technology Library in Gothenburg, Sweden.

Fjallbrant, Nancy. *NVBF Anglo--Scandinavian Seminar on Library User Education. Proceedings.* Gothenburg, Sweden: Chalmers University of Technology Library, 1977.

These proceedings are based on a seminar on user education held November 2--4, 1976 in Sweden. 14 participants presented papers on the role of the academic library, library instruction in Denmark, Finland, Norway, Sweden, and the United Kingdom. Also covered were topics like communication, teaching methods, audio-visual materials and evaluation of user instruction.

Fjallbrant, Nancy. "Planning a Programme of Library User Education." *Journal of Librarianship.* 9 (1977), pp. 199--211.

"Guidelines for Bibliographic Instruction in Academic Libraries." *College and Research Libraries News.* 38 (April, 1977), p. 92.

Gives a copy of the guidelines developed by ACRL Bibliographic Instruction Task Force after their approval as policy by the ACRL Board of Directors on January 31, 1977.

Hall, Audrey W. "One Use of Audio--Cassettes for Library Instruction." *Education Libraries Bulletin.* 20 (1977), p. 29--31.

Advantages of the use of audio cassettes in library

instruction are discussed. Some problems in utilizing this method are pointed out and solutions to overcome them are given.

Hardesty, Larry. "Use of Slide–Tape Presentations in Academic Libraries: A State–of–the–Art Survey." *Journal of Academic Librarians.* 3 (July, 1977), pp. 135–140.

This is a summary of a survey of 258 slide–tape programs used in academic library instruction conducted by the author. It was found that there is much duplication among libraries in this area, that the production of good programs takes special expertise, time and money.

Harris, Colin. "Educating the User." *Library Association Record.* 79 (July, 1977), pp. 359–360.

The author feels that academic libraries fall into 5 groups in their attitude to library instruction. Most librarians fall into the group that feel they need to provide the library instruction and try to do the best they can in spite of many obstacles. The author feels that some help for these librarians is available in the form of the British Travelling Workshop Experiment and the "learning packages" developed through them.

Harris, Colin. "Illuminative Evaluation of User Education Programmes." *Aslib Proceedings.* 10 (October, 1977) pp. 348–362.

This describes an evaluation method in user education called "illuminative evaluation." Its uses and components are explained and an evaluation checklist is appended.

Houghton, B. "Whatever Happened to Tutor Librarianship?" *Art Library Journal.* 1 (Winter, 1976) pp. 4–19.

The article discusses tutor librarianship at the Leicester Polytechnic, the results and problems connected with it and some suggestions for improving any disadvantages which resulted from creating the tutor librarian as a separate position.

Kirkendall, Carolyn. "Library Instruction: A Column of Opinion." *Journal of Academic Librarianship.* 3 (March, 1977), pp. 34–35.

This column is concerned with the use of audio–visual materials in library instruction. Opinions are given from five librarians at MIT, the University of South Florida, North Dakota State University and UCLA.

Kirkendall, Carolyn. "Library Instruction: A Column of Opinion." *Journal of Academic Librarianship.* 3 (May, 1977), pp. 94–95.

This column addressed itself to the issue of under-graduate library skills courses and their effectiveness in meeting students' needs. Five opinions from practicing library instruction librarians demonstrate the profession's divided views on this.

Kirkendall, Carolyn. "Library Instruction: A Column of Opinion." *Journal of Academic Librarianship.* 3 (July, 1977), pp. 154--155.

The question dealing with current prime concerns of practicing library instruction librarians was answered by librarians from five institutions -- Brigham Young, University of Michigan, Occidental College, Earlham College and Lawrence University.

Kirkendall, Carolyn. "Library Instruction: A Column of Opinion." *Journal of Academic Librarianship.* 3 (September, 1977), pp. 214--215.

This column presents reactions and responses to previous columns by seven academic librarians.

Kirkendall, Carolyn. "Library Instruction: A Column of Opinion." *Journal of Academic Librarianship.* 3 (November, 1977), pp. 288--289.

This column asks for opinions on how effective user education can be improved. Five promoters of library instruction respond from the University of Pretoria, University of Pennsylvania, Cedar Crest and Muhlenberg Colleges, University of Toronto and the University of North Carolina.

Lenski, S. "Library Orientation -- A Way of Hope for Users and Staff." *Illinois Libraries.* 59 (April, 1977), pp. 293--295.

Subject--oriented workshops for all students in known library--use problem areas were developed at Boston University. Most of the staff was involved in developing these workshops which seem an effective way for user education.

"Library Use Instruction in Academic and Research Libraries." *ARL Management Supplement.* 5 (September, 1977) 6p.

This monograph assesses the current state of library use instruction in academic libraries and provides reasons for the recent growth in this area of library service. Different phases of library use instruction programs are discussed based on a survey of ARL member libraries and 30 additional academic libraries.

Lynch, Sister Dennis. "U.S. by Bus: or What Is Going On

in B.I. Land?" Viewpoints, *Catholic Library World.* 49 (October, 1977), pp. 136–137.

    The first of seven proposed columns on bibliographic instruction in U.S. academic libraries. Discusses the library instruction movement in relationship to ALA, ACRL and Project LOEX.

Lynch, Sister Dennis. "College, University and Seminary Libraries." *Catholic Library World.* 49 (November, 1977), pp. 184–186.

    In the second of seven columns on Sister Dennis' summary of her U.S. by Bus survey on library instruction, she discusses academic library instruction activities in the Seventies. She includes information about conferences, grant programs and type of library instruction.

Lynch, Sister Dennis. "U.S. by Bus: No. 3," 'Viewpoints.' *Catholic Library World.* 49 (December, 1977), pp. 225–226.

    In the third column Sister Dennis discusses instructional materials used in various libraries for library use instruction.

MacGregor, John and Raymond G. McInnis. "Integrating Classroom Instruction and Library Research." *Journal of Higher Education.* 48 (January–February, 1977), pp. 17–38.

    This paper discusses a structural–functional approach to library literature searches, relates that approach to a theory of the epistemological structure of knowledge, outlines a recommended sequence of steps to be followed in typical research efforts and demonstrates graphically the kind of results which can be obtained through this method. The results of this method are a highly efficient mode of research, an enriching classroom experience, and a mode of learning for students to enrich their future lives.

Marshall, A.P. "This Teaching/Learning Thing: Librarians as Educators." *Academic Libraries by the Year 2000,* edited by Herbert Poole. New York: Bowker, 1977, pp. 50–63.

    The author discusses academic librarians' involvement in the instructional process in the 60's and 70's, support funding for these activities from the Council on Library Resources, the mission of higher education and how librarians fit into it.

Miller, Lawrence. "Liaison Work in the Academic Library." *RQ.* 16 (Spring, 1977), pp. 213–215.

The author discusses librarian–faculty cooperation in academic libraries and gives some suggestions and techniques for developing such cooperation.

Oakley, Adeline. *Content Analysis of Student Responses in Topic–Centered Library Orientation.* Phd Dissertation, Boston University, School of Education, 1977.

This study attempts to establish more precise measures of library skills by investigating links between tests of library proficiency and tests predicting academic success, and between paper and pencil tests and hands–on use of reference sources. Reliability for topic–centered search strategy exercises as criteria for measuring library skills were determined. A machine–scorable diagnostic test for college freshmen was devised.

Patterson, Margaret C. "Library Literacy–A Cumulative Experience." *Literary Research Newsletter.* 2 (October, 1977), pp. 180–186.

Cooperation or lack of it between librarians and professors is discussed here. It is advocated that more literary scholars with an understanding of librarianship and more librarians who are scholars are needed. Both teachers and librarians need to cooperate for the most effective teaching.

Pearce, B.L. "Tuition in Library Use as a Part of Open University Preparatory Courses." *Library Review.* 25 (Autumn, 1976), pp. 254–256.

The author discusses the necessity for library use instruction to students enrolled in Open University programs in the United Kingdom. An outline for such a library instruction program is also included.

"The President Views the Campus Library." *Journal of Academic Librarianship.* 3 (September, 1977), pp. 192–199.

Eight presidents of academic institutions present their opinions on their campus libraries. They express concern about financing the library, collection building, use of the library, faculty status for librarians and library instruction.

Rader, Hannelore B. *Library Instruction in the Seventies: State of the Art.* Papers Presented at the Sixth Annual Conference on Library Orientation for Academic Libraries held at Eastern Michigan University, May 13–14, 1976. Ann Arbor, Pierian Press, 1977.

This volume includes papers by ten library instruction practitioners on the state of the art in library use instruction in Canada, the Middle East, on credit courses, course–

related instruction, Project LOEX, Eastern Michigan University's program and evaluation of library instruction.

Rawlinson, Stephen. "A Role for the Academic Library in Library Instruction." *Physics Education.* 12 (1977), pp. 432--433.

    Discusses the need for user instruction for science students in cooperation with faculty and related to coursework.

Sandock, Mollie. "A Study of University Students' Awareness of Reference Services." *RQ.* 16 (1977), pp. 284--296.

Schwob, E. "Orientation: Library Program Shows Gratifying Results." *Feliciter.* 23 (February, 1977), p. 3.

    Discusses library instruction at the University of Alberta to English students. It utilizes a lesson plan and a kit of information for each student.

Shain, Charles H. "Filming Narrative" for Library Instruction Film "You Don't Have to Be a Hero to Use the U.C. Library." 1976. 32p. ED 134 215.

    Described here is the process of making a 13-minute, super 8 film for formal library instruction at the University of California, Berkeley. Script, budget, field tests and evaluation results are included.

Smalley, Topsy N. "Bibliographic Instruction in Academic Libraries: Questioning Some Assumptions." *Journal of Academic Librarianship.* 3 (November, 1977), pp. 280--283.

    This article discusses some problems in the teaching of library skills such as librarians are not teaching conceptual library skills but rather technical ones. It is advocated that theories of learning should be applied to develop a conceptual framework for development of library researching skills.

Stevenson, M.B. *User Education Programmes: A Study of Their Development, Organization, Methods and Assessment.* British Library Research and Development Department Reports, 1977.

    This is a study and a survey of user education programmes in higher education libraries in the United Kingdom completed during April--October, 1975. It discusses objectives, orientation, bibliographic instruction, evaluation, problems and future trends.

Stoffle, Carla and Julie Larson. "Academic Library Skills, How 10 Wisconsin Academic Libraries Teach Library Use?" *Wisconsin Library Bulletin.* (July--August, 1977), pp. 157--158.

This summarizes library instruction activities in Wisconsin academic libraries and highlights specific instructional activities.

Stoffle, Carla and J. Pryor. "Parkside Teaches Library Use from Orientation to Competency Requirments." *Wisconsin Library Bulletin.* (July--August, 1977), pp. 159--160.

This is a short description of the library use instruction program carried out at the University of Wisconsin--Parkside campus. A more detailed description can be found in ED 126 973.

Tucker, John M. "An Experiment in Bibliographic Instruction at Wabash College." *College and Research Libraries.* 38 (May, 1977), pp. 203--209.

This is a condensed version of the five-year report on the Wabash College 5--year bibliographic instruction program guided by faculty by the NEH--CLR. Specially trained student assistants were utilized to instruct others in library skills.

Vuturo, R. "Beyond the Library Tour: Those Who Can, Must Teach." *Wilson Library Bulletin.* 51 (May, 1977), pp. 736--740.

Advocates that academic librarians become more involved in the instructional process by providing necessary library use instruction. Gives an overview of possible uses of media in library use instruction.

Vuturo, R.A. and C. Cowdrick. "Recycling the College Library." *College Composition and Communication.* 28 (February, 1977), pp. 57--58.

The article discusses the problem of library instruction to college freshmen as provided by the English faculty. It is suggested that surplus library materials (catalog cards, superseded indexes and abstracts) could be moved into the classroom to provide hands--on experience for students. Also suggested is that students could be provided with sets of questions relating to these materials to give them practical application in using them.

Wilkinson, E.H. and others. *The Use of a University Library's Subject Catalogue: Report of a Research Project.* 1977. 99p. ED 142 231.

This is a report on the development and evaluations of a library instruction program designed to teach students the effective use of the subject catalog at the Macquarie University in Australia. Objectives, two teaching methods and three evaluation instruments are described. All supportive materials and references are appended.

Wilson, J.H. "Librarian: Introverted or Intregrated." *Australian Academic and Research Libraries.* 8 (June, 1977) pp. 87–93.

PUBLIC LIBRARIES

Rishoj, Jorgen. "Library Guidance for the Public and Library PR as Seen from Bibliotekscentralen." *Scandinavian Public Library Quarterly.* 10 (1977) pp. 46–51.

    An active centralized public relations program for Danish public libraries is discussed in detail. Such a program will help to orient and guide the public library user.

SCHOOL LIBRARIES

Chedsey, K.A. "All about the Library." *Instructor.* 87 (November, 1977), pp. 124–5.

    Outlines some ideas for orienting very young children to the library, especially the children's room.

Clark, M.W. "Toot – Toot for Reading." *Instructor.* 87 (November, 1977), p. 47.

Clarke, Penelope. "Working Together: Cooperation between Teachers and Librarians in the Field of School Libraries." *The School Librarian.* 25 (December, 1977), pp. 319–327.

    This discusses areas of cooperation between teachers and librarians in schools on book selection, curriculum, meetings, instructing students in library use and so on. Some suggestions for developing such cooperation are provided.

Conor, R. "New Slant on YA Service." *Focus.* 31 (May, 1977), p. 6.

Dermon, E.S. "Getting to Know the Library." *Media and Methods.* 13 (April, 1977), p. 54.

    A high school English teacher bemoans the fact that today's students seem to have little or no interest in libraries. To remedy this situation with his own students he devised a worksheet to help students teach themselves about the use of the library. The worksheet is included.

Fisher, Denise R. *A Study of the Library Skills Instruction of Entering Freshmen to St. Francis Seminary High School.* Master Thesis, 1976. ED 130 670. 53p.

This is a study of 40 students and the 61 elementary and secondary schools they attended previously to assess their library skills knowledge and the library skills pro-grams offered at those schools. Appended are a biblio-graphy and an evaluation instrument.

Grant, L.T. "Library Lesson, Constructed on Piagetian Princi-ples, for Use in Self--Service Elementary Instructional Media Centers." *Texas Library Journal.* 53 (Winter, 1977), pp. 24--7.

The author discusses library skills program for each level in elementary school based on Piagetian principles. Theoretical and practical information is included as well as a sample library lesson for second grade.

Hamilton, Linda. "Suggestions for Secondary School Library Lessons." *School Librarian.* 25 (September, 1977), pp. 217--220.

The author, a teacher--librarian at Billericay School in Essex, U.K., comments on how the "library lesson" can be used in a more constructive manner to teach useful skills in secondary schools. A timetable and activities are detailed.

Hein, C.E. "Independent Study Guides: Mann Junior High Students Learn Library Media Skills." *Wisconsin Library Bulletin.* 73 (May, 1977), pp. 129--30.

Humes, Barbara. "Elementary Students." *Audiovisual Instruc--tion.* 22 (December, 1977), pp. 28--29.

Describes a project with fifth graders who were trained to do a research project similar to that required for a college paper.

Hyland, A. "Instructional Standards." *Ohio Association of School Libraries Bulletin.* 28 (October, 1976), pp. 36--9. (Joint issue with *Educational Media in Ohio*).

Kouns, B. "Thirteen Steps to Library Orientation." *School Library Journal.* 23 (March, 1977), p. 125.

Describes a library orientation program in Santa Teresa High School which is organized around a slide--tape presentation, tests, worksheets, teacher manuals and evaluation, in thirteen steps.

Mattleman, Marciene S. and Howard E. Blake. "Study Skills: Prescriptions for Survival." *Language Arts.* 54 (Novem--ber/December, 1977), pp. 925--927.

The article provides some guidance to teachers in the area of helping students develop study skills including information gathering skills by suggesting some practical applications of these skills.

"Nevada High Schoolers Get University Orientation." *Library Journal.* 102 (August, 1977), p. 1552.

Reports that high school students can take the University of Nevada's Introduction to the Library Course. Upper level students can get university credit for it.

Nording, Jo Anne. *Dear Faculty: A Discovery Method Guidebook to the High School Library.* Westwood, Mass.: Faxon, Inc. (1976).

This work is intended for individual and group library use instruction and is planned to overcome the problems of limited resources and teaching library skills in a vacuum. Clear guidelines, thorough lesson plans and some humor make this a most useful manual for all high school librarians.

Stagg, Sylvia and Sarah Brew. "Finding the Book You Want: An Algorithm." *School Librarian.* 25 (September, 1977), pp. 221--222.

A flow-chart for finding books in the junior high level libraries is described in this brief article by librarians from the Seven Oaks School in Kent, U.K.

Waltzer, Margaret A. "Library Instruction in Secondary Schools." *Catholic Library World.* 48 (April, 1977), pp. 402--403.

The author bemoans the fact that high school students seem to receive inadequate library skills instruction at the present time. She outlines the library science course taught at her school, the Dominican High School in New Orleans.

Wehmeyer, Lillian B. *The School Librarian as Educator.* Littleton, Col.: Libraries Unlimited, Inc., 1976.

The purpose of this book is to help school librarians become true educators by providing them with educational theory and research to prepare them for the teaching role. In order for the school librarian to fulfill this role he or she needs to know the principles of educational psychology and learning theories as well as instructional techniques. The book provides such information and much more in an effort to prepare librarians to teach students and teachers. Many games, learning activities and suggestions are included.

Winkworth, F.V. *User Education in Schools.* A Survey of the Literature on Education for Library and Information Use in Schools. Report to British Library Research and Development Department. May, 1977.

Examination of recent British and American informa--

tion on library user education in schools was examined and theoretical as well as practical factors to help in planning such programs have been extracted. Recommendations for library skills programs in schools and for further research are included. An annotated bibliography is appended.

SPECIAL LIBRARIES AND GROUPS

Bowen, A.M. "On-line Literature Retrieval as a Continuing Medical Education Course." *Medical Library Association Bulletin.* 65 (July, 1977), pp. 384-386.

Davis, Elizabeth B. and others. "Two-Phased Model for Library Instruction." *Medical Library Association Bulletin.* (January, 1977), pp. 40-51.

This gives a description of two different methods for library orientation and instruction -- individualized audio-print orientation and computer-assisted instruction using PLATO. Evaluations by users have encouraged the librarians to continue these methods.

Hall, Darielle. "A Library Training Program for Native Americans." *Wilson Library Bulletin.* 51 (May, 1977), pp. 751-754.

Describes a 6-week course for Native Americans to train them in library know-how, including selection, cataloging, circulation of print and non-print materials etc. The object of the training was to provide them with the ability to run tribal libraries and information centers.

Lipow, Anne G. "User Education and Publicity for On-Line Services." *On-Line Bibliographic Services. Where We Are Where We're Going.* Edited by Peter G. Watson. Chicago: ALA, 1977. pp. 67-71.

How to publicize a computerized literature search service and how to educate its potential library user effectively are the topics discussed in this chapter. Because computer searches will cost the patrons something, it is most important to provide them with information as to what exactly they will get for their money. Appended are some publicity materials.

Peck, Theodore. "The Engineering Library as an Applied Learning Laboratory." *Engineering Education.* 67 (1977), pp. 723-724.

Poyer, R.K. "Improved Library Services through User Education." *Medical Library Association Bulletin.* 65 (April,

1977), pp. 296–297.

    This article discusses a short library skills course for allied health personnel at the Medical University of South Carolina which involves four 2-hour sessions.

Proceedings of the Seminar on User Education Activities, the State of the Art in Texas. (Houston, Texas, April, 1976). 1977. 43p. ED 138 247.

    Includes 6 papers on user education in school, academic, public and special libraries. Also included are a bibliography and summaries of surveys in these types of libraries.

Rutstein, Joel S. *Access to U.S. Government Statistics through Course-Related Instruction.* 1976. 17p. ED 134 211.

    At the Colorado State University Libraries a self-guided exercise to teach the use of the *Monthly Catalog* and *American Statistics Index* was developed. Practical application material for students is included.

Walser, Katina P. and K.W. Kruse. "A College Course for Nurses on the Utilization of Library Resources." *Medical Library Association Bulletin.* 65 (April, 1977), pp. 265–267.

    A ten week 1½ credit course on library skills for nursing students is being offered at Duke University to teach them library know-how in their subject field.

Whitbeck, George W. and Hernon Peter. "Bibliographic Instruction in Government Publications: Lecture Programs and Their Evaluation in American Academic Depository Libraries." *Government Publications Review.* 4 (1977), pp. 1–12.

    The article is based on responses to a questionnaire from 97 academic depository libraries. It was found that the use of government publications needs more promoting. Among the promotion and educational methods for these publications, library class lectures are utilized most often in an outreach effort to library users. Lecture effectiveness tends to be evaluated more than any other instructional effort.

Woolpy, J.H. "Information Retrieval for Introductory Science Courses." *American Biology Teacher.* 29 (March, 1977), pp. 162–164.

    The Earlham College library instruction program in the sciences is discussed by one of the biology professors involved in this program. The library component of the general biology course is described in detail as to teaching methods, exercises, testing and student reactions. It is pointed out that the attitude of the teachers and librarians are most important for the success of such a program.

ALL LEVELS

Ardhanareeswaran, B. "Reference Skills and Education for Development." *Journal of Reading.* 20 (May, 1977), pp. 674--676.

    The author bemoans the fact that in India students on all levels do not learn sufficient library skills especially as related to the study of the English language. Library-centered education featuring the utilization of reference sources is advocated.

Batt, Fred. "Education Is Illogical." *Improving College and University Teaching.* 25 (Summer, 1977), p. 188.

    The author advocates complete integration of the library into the educational process through total cooperation between information specialists, teaching and research faculty. This would bring about the "real" education of all students.

Berry, John. "The Two 'Professions'." *Library Journal.* 102 (September, 1977), p. 1699.

    This editorial discusses the missions of the library professional, one of which is to teach users how to obtain needed information skills. It urges librarians to continue that mission.

Droog, Jan. "Education of the Information User." *International Forum on Information and Documentation.* 1 (1976) pp. 26--32.

    The author introduces a pilot project to educate information users at all educational levels from elementary through academic faculty. Reasons and objectives for user education are provided, the state of user education in some countries is summarized and a suggested outline for the proposed program is provided.

Kirk, Thomas. "Past, Present and Future of Library Instruction." *Southeastern Librarian.* 27 (Spring, 1977), pp. 15--18.

    This article reviews briefly the history of library use instruction in all types of libraries and gives some predictions for future trends and development in this area.

Phillips, L. "Making Library Instruction More Palatable." *American Vocational Journal.* 52 (April, 1977), pp. 57--58.

Rosenblum, Joseph. "The Future of Reference Service: Death by Complexity." *Wilson Library Bulletin.* 52 (December, 1977), pp. 300–1+.

    The author discusses the increasing complexities of information sources and the difficulties in teaching library users retrieval methods. He feels that simplification of reference sources is needed and that librarians should play a strong role in bringing about such simplification through working more closely with publishers and authors.

Spaulding, Carl. "Teaching the Use of Microfilm Readers." *Microform Review.* 6 (March, 1977), pp. 80–81.

    The article describes techniques for training staff and teaching library users the operations of microfilm readers. A manual should be part of the training program.

Stevenson, Malcolm. "Progress in Documentation. Education of Users of Libraries and Information Services." *Journal of Documentation.* 33 (March, 1977), pp. 53–78.

    Provides an overview of user education in the United Kingdom, the United States, and other countries. Discusses different phases and aspects of user education. Includes information on different types of libraries, objectives and evaluation of programs.

Suzuki, Yukishisa. "Library Services: Education for Librarians and Library Users in a Multi--Lingual Multi--Ethnic Environment." *Proceedings of IFLA Worldwide Seminar, May 31–June 2,* Korean Library Association, 1976. pp. 96–101.

EIGHTH ANNUAL CONFERENCE
ON
LIBRARY ORIENTATION
FOR
ACADEMIC LIBRARIES

EASTERN MICHIGAN UNIVERSITY
May 4 & 5, 1978

REGISTRANTS

Adams, Mignon
Coor. Lib. Inst.
Penfield Library
State College of New York
Oswego, NY 16126

Ahmad, Carol
Asst. Human. Libr.
Oklahoma State University
Stillwater, OK 74074

Alleman, David
Ref. Libr.
Hillsdale College
Hillsdale, MI 49242

Allen, Ronald
Ref./Instr. Libr.
Wayne State University
Detroit, MI 48202

Allen, Sandra
Instruction Libr.
University of Minnesota
Minneapolis, MN 55455

Anders, Vicki
Instr. Services Libr.
Texas A & M University
College Station, TX 77843

Andrews, Ann
Education Specialist
Eastern Michigan University
Ypsilanti, MI 48197

Andrews, Phyllis
Asst. Ref. Libr.
University of Rochester
Rochester, NY 14627

Arguello de Cardona, Marla
Library Director
Universidad Interamericana
San Juan, Puerto Rico 00919

Atkins, Thomas V.
Chief--Instr. Serv.
Baruch College -- CUNY
New York, NY 10010

Aulds, Ellen Lou
IMC Libr.
Miami University
Oxford, OH 45056

Barnes, Michelle
Sec. -- Project LOEX
Eastern Michigan University
Ypsilanti, MI 48197

Babel, Rayonia A.
Ref. Libr.
Aurora College
Aurora, IL 60507

Beaubien, Anne
Ref. Libr./Bibliog. Instr.
Graduate Library
University of Michigan
Ann Arbor, MI 48109

Belanger, Mae D.
Serials Libr.
Ohio Dominican College
Columbus, OH 43219

Berge, Pat
Libr.
Univ. of Wisconsin -- Parkside
Kenosha, WI 43151

Beyerlein, Lydia
Asst. Ref. Libr.
Johns Hopkins University
Baltimore, MD 21218

Binkowski, Laura
Asst. Libr.
Columbia University
New York, NY 10027

Birge, Ilene A.
Ref. Libr.
Indiana University -- SB
South Bend, IN 46615

Books, Nancy
Head -- Ref. Dept.
Bucknell University
Lewisburg, PA 17837

Bowen, Albertine C.
Assoc. Dir. -- Media Center
University of District Columbia
Washington, DC 20001

Brennan, David K.
Law Librarian
University of Alabama
Tuscaloosa, AL 35486

Brennan, Exir B.
Coord. -- Library Instr.
University of Alabama
Tuscaloosa, AL 35486

Byrd, Theresa
Ref. Libr.
J. Sargeant Reynolds
  Community College
Richmond, VA 23241

Cain, Melissa
Asst. Underg. Libr.
University of Illinois
Urbana, IL 61801

Cappuzzello, Paul G.
Instr. Libr.
University of Toledo
Toledo, OH 43606

Cevallos, Elena
Ref./Instr. Libr.
Hofstra University
Hempstead, NY 11550

Cipolla, Katherine G.
Media Serv. Libr.
MIT -- Barker Engin. Library
Cambridge, MA 02130

Clark, Carolyn
P.O. Box 1391
West Stadium Blvd.
Ann Arbor, MI 48106

Collins, John W.
LSEP Project Director
Glenville State College
Glenville, WV 26351

Coniglio, Jamie Wright
Info. Serv. Libr.
Bradley University
Peoria, IL 61625

Covington, Paula A.
LSEP Coordinator
Joint University Libraries
Nashville, TN 37215

Coyne, Martin
Proj. Libr./Lib. Or.
Case Western Reserve University
Cleveland, OH 44106

Cragg, Carole
Ref. Libr.
Trinity College
Deerfield, IL 60015

Cravey, Pamela
LSEP Libr.
Georgia State University
Atlanta, GA 30303

Culbertson, Margaret
Coord. -- User Education
University of Houston
Houston, TX 77004

Cuthbertson, Ann
Asst. Head Undergr. Libr.
Indiana University
Bloomington, IN 47401

Czisny, Julie
Coord. -- Media Resources
University of Wisconsin
Milwaukee, WI 53201

Deering, Ronald F.
Librarian
Southern Baptist Theological
 Seminary
Louisville, KY 40206

Demas, Sam
Circ. Reserve & Instr.
Cornell University
Ithaca, NY 14850

Dennett, Louise K.
Ill./Orient Librarian
Northeastern University
Boston, MA 02115

DeVinney, Gemma
Ref. Libr.
UGL -- SUNY at Buffalo
Buffalo, NY 14214

Dickerson, Lynn
Professor of English
University of Richmond
Richmond, VA 23173

Dittman, Maria
Ref. Libr.
Marquette University
Milwaukee, WI 53233

Dudley, Miriam
Coord. Publ. Serv./Lib. Inst.
UCLA
Los Angeles, CA 90024

Duesbury, Gail M.
Info. Serv. Libr.
University of Wisconsin
LaCrosse, WI 54601

Durnell, Jane B.
Coord. Lib. Inst.
University of Oregon
Eugene, OR 97403

Dusenbury, Carolyn
Instr. Libr.
University of Utah
Salt Lake City, UT 84112

DuVal, Kate
Librarian
University of Richmond
Richmond, VA 23173

Edwards, LeRoy
Dir. -- Instr. Services
Central State University
Wilberforce, OH 45384

Eisenberg, Phyllis
Ref. Libr.
Piedmond Virginia
  Community College
Charlottesville, VA 22901

Elkins, Elizabeth
Assoc. Libr.
SUNY -- Sci. & Forestry
Syracuse, NY 13210

Ellis, Elizabeth
Coord. -- Instr. Programs
Pennsylvania State University
University Park, PA 16802

Espo, Hal
Asst. to Exec. Sec.
Assoc. of Col. & Research Libs.
Chicago, IL 60611

Evans, Anita
Asst. Humanities Librarian
Oklahoma State University
Stillwater, OK 74074

Evans, John E.
Ref. Libr.
University of South Dakota
Vermillion, SD 57069

Evans, Marilyn
Acting Head -- Publ. Serv.
Baldwin--Wallace College
Berea, OH 44017

Farmer, Ruth B.
Acquis. Librarian
University of Central Arkansas
Conway, AR 72032

Faust, Margaret S.
Ref. Libr.
Stephens College
Columbia, MO 65211

Fennessy, Kathryn
Ref. Libr.
Alfred University
Alfred, NY 14802

Flower, Kam
Ref. Libr.
University of Maine
Orono, ME 04473

Foster, Jocelyn
Information Librarian
University of British Columbia
Vancouver, BC CANADA

Fox, Mary Anne
Asst. Ref. Libr.
Southern Illinois University
Carbondale, IL 62901

Fox, Peter K.
Ref. Libr.
Cambridge University
Cambridge, England

Frank, Virginia
Ref./Instr.
Millikin University
Decatur, IL 62522

Freedman, Janet
Publ. Serv. Libr.
Salem State College
Salem, MA 01970

Frick, Elizabeth
Head -- User Serv.
University of Colorado
Colorado Springs, CO 80907

Fricke, Benno G.
Dir. -- Eval. & Exam. Office
University of Michigan
Ann Arbor, MI 48109

Frontz, Stephanie
Fine Arts Librarian
University of Rochester
Rochester, NY 14627

Frost, William J.
Ref. Libr.
Bloomsburg State College
Bloomsburg, PA 17815

Fulton, William R.
Ref. Libr.
Pennsylvania State University
Monaca, PA 15061

Gadsden, Alice
Ref. Libr.
University of South Carolina
Greensboro, NC 27412

George, Mary
Bibliog. Instr./Ref. Libr.
Graduate Library
University of Michigan
Ann Arbor, MI 48109

Gerity, Louise P.
Bibliog. Instr. Libr.
Lewis & Clark College
Portland, OR 97219

Gillespie, David
Director -- Kidd Library
Glenville State College
Glenville, WV 26351

Goodstein, Sylvia
Ref. Libr.
Montgomery County College
Rockville, MD 20850

Groesbeck, Margaret
Ref./Instr. Serv. Librarian
Amherst College
Amherst, MA 01002

Gwinn, Nancy E.
Info. & Publications Officer
Council on Library Resources
Washington, DC 20036

Hahn, Ruth
Reader Services Librarian
Indiana State University
Evansville, IN 47712

Harrison, Orion
LSEP Project Librarian
Georgia Southern College
Statesboro, GA 30458

Hart, Elaine
Instr. Libr.
DePaul University
Chicago, IL 60604

Hartley, Debra
Publ. Services Librarian
Wartburg College
Waverly, IO 50677

Head, Judy
Head -- Admin. Studies Library
University of Manitoba
Winnipeg, CANADA R3T2N2

Healy, Barbara
Asst. Management Librarian
University of Rochester
Rochester, NY 14627

Hendricks, Dwight T.
Assoc. Head -- Library
Hiram College
Hiram, OH 44234

Herbison, Michael
Director -- Library
University of Colorado
Colorado Springs, CO 80907

Herndon, Gail
Ref. Libr.
Ohio State University
Columbus, OH 43201

Hill, Denny
Inst. of Soc.
Georgia Southern College
Statesboro, GA 30458

Hogan, Sharon
Ref. Libr./Bibliog. Instr.
Graduate Library
University of Michigan
Ann Arbor, MI 48109

Holley, Edward G.
Dean -- Library School
University of North Carolina
Chapel Hill, NC 27514

Hoover, Alice
Ref. Libr.
Ball State University
Muncie, IN 47306

Hosel, Harry
Coord. -- Lib. Instr.
University of California
Riverside, CA 92507

Hubble, Gerald B.
Library Director
Rockhurst College
Kansas City, MO 64110

Hudson, Phyllis J.
Assoc. Libr.
Florida Technological University
Orlando, FL 32816

Hughes, Phyllis
Instr. Services Libr.
Berea College
Berea, KY 40404

Huling, Nancy
Instr./Ref. Librarian
SUNY
Binghamton, NY 13901

Hutchins, Carol
Ref. Libr.
University of New Mexico
Albuquerque, NM 87131

Jackson, James
Librarian
University of Richmond
Richmond, VA 23173

Johnson, Jean S.
Coord. -- Pub. Services
University of Wyoming
Laramie, WY 82071

Jordan, Janis
Instr. Serv. Libr.
Sangamon State University
Springfield, IL 62708

Kasalko, Sally
Ref. Libr.
Med. & Health Related Sci.
Little Rock, AR 72201

Keever, Ellen
Andrews Library
College of Wooster
Wooster, OH 44691

Kinderski, Judy
Ref. Libr.
St. Cloud State University
St. Cloud, MN 56301

King, Judith D.
Ref. Libr.
Grand Valley State College
Allendale, MI 49401

Kirk, Thomas
Science Librarian
Earlham College
Richmond, IN 47374

Kirkendall, Carolyn
Director -- Project LOEX
Eastern Michigan University
Ypsilanti, MI 48197

Kirkpatrick, Nancy
Publ. Serv. Librarian
Yavapai College
Prescott, AZ 86301

Koyama, Janice
Coor. -- Ref./Instr. Serv.
California State University
Long Beach, CA 90840

Kraft, Lillian
Asst. Prof. -- Lib. Instr.
Iowa State University
Ames, IO 50010

Kratz, Abby
Women's Studies Lib.
Ohio State University
Columbus, OH 43210

LaRose, Al
Head -- Ref. Dept.
Wittenberg, University
Springfield, OH 45501

Laughlin, Steven G.
Ref./Bib. for Business
University of Alabama
Birmingham, AL 35294

Lee, Jo Ann
Head -- Reader Serv.
Lake Forest College
Lake Forest, IL 60045

Levin, Ellen
Reader Serv. Libr.
Framingham State College
Framingham, MA 01701

Lewis, Helen
Ref. Libr.
University of Connecticut
Storrs, CT 06268

Lincoln, John
Ref. Libr.
Lansing Community College
Lansing, MI 48901

Lindgren, Susan L.
Ref. Libr.
University of Vermont
Burlington, VT 05401

Lippincott, Joan K.
Ref. Libr.
SUNY
Brockport, NY 14420

Long, Caroline C.
Documents Librarian
Franklin & Marshall College
Lancaster, PA 17604

McAndrew, Patricia A.
Publ. Serv. Librarian
University of Virginia
Charlottesville, VA 22901

McClaskey, Karen
Ref. Libr.
School of the Ozarks
Pt. Lookout, MO 65726

McDonald, Mary
Library
Univ. of Wisconsin – Parkside
Kenosha, WI 43151

McGuire, Maribeth
Instructor of English
Tusculum College
Greeneville, TN 37743

McIntyre, C. Burnelle
Orient./Instr. Libr.
Gallaudet College
Washington, DC 20002

McNamara, Martha
Librarian
Boston College
Chestnut Hill, MA 02167

Mader, Sharon B.
Ref. Libr.
Lake Forest College
Lake Forest, IL 60045

Mancuso, Mary
Ref. Libr./Humanities
University of Evansville
Evansville, IN 47702

Margutti, Elizabeth
Asst. Ge'l Ref. Libr.
Virginia Polytechnic Institute &
 State University
Blacksburg, VA 24060

Marshall, A.P.
Ref. Libr.
Eastern Michigan University
Ypsilanti, MI 48197

Martinez, Christina
User Serv. Libr.
University of Colorado
Colorado Springs, CO 80907

Masters, Deborah C.
Ref. Libr.
Pennsylvania State University
University Park, PA 16802

Maughan, Laurel S.
Lib. Instr. Libr.
Oregon State University
Corvallis, OR 97330

Meadows, Janice
Director – LRC
Eastern Shore Community
 College
Melfa, VA 23410

Meahl, Darren
Underg. a–v Librarian
Michigan State University
East Lansing, MI 48824

Meloy, Patricia
Ref. Libr.
Barat College
Lake Forest, IL 60045

Meyer, Wayne
LSEP Librarian
Beloit College
Beloit, WI 53511

Mickelson, Shirley A.
Ref. Libr.
University of Missouri
Kansas City, MO 64110

Millis, Cherry
Coord. -- Publ. Serv.
James Madison University
Harrisonburg, VA 22801

Miner, Mary Gabrielle
Publ. Serv. Libr.
Central State University
Wilberforce, OH 45384

Miya, Mary Ann
History/Soc. Bibliog.
Loyola University
Chicago, IL 60626

Morgan, Eloise
LSEP Project Librarian
Hampton Institute
Hampton, VA 23668

Mosby, Margaret A.
Asst. Ref. Libr.
MCV Station -- Box 667
Richmond, VA 23298

Murray, Carolyn
Coor. -- Lib. Instr.
University of Toronto
Toronto, Ontario, CANADA
M3C 1E6

Myers, Georgianna
Ref./Instr. Libr.
University of Wisconsin
Whitewater, WI 53190

Myers, Susan
LSEP Project Librarian
Colorado College
Colorado Springs, CO 80903

Nagpal, Regina
Asst. Ref. Libr.
Wittenberg University
Springfield, OH 45501

Nicholson, Barbara E.
Asst. Dir. -- Read. Serv.
Miami University
Oxford, OH 45056

Niederboin, Annette
Librarian
Western Wisconsin Tech. Institute
LaCrosse, WI 54601

Noble, Eleanor
Director
University of Albuquerque
Albuquerque, NM 87140

Nunnelei, Janice L.
Ref. Libr.
Southeast MO State University
Cape Girardeau, MO 63701

Nye, James
Reader Serv. Libr.
Gustaf Adolphus College
St. Peter, MN 56082

Nyitray, Nancy
Librarian
St. Clair County Community
  College
Port Huron, MI 48060

Oberman-Soroka, Cerise
Ref. Libr.
College of Charleston
Charleston, SC 29403

Olevnik, Peter P.
Head of Reference
SUNY
Brockport, NY 14420

Oltman, Jerilyn K.
Instr. Serv. Libr.
Carl Sandburg College
Galesburg, IL 61401

Pastine, Maureen
Undergraduate Librarian
University of Illinois
Urbana, IL 61801

Pearson, Penny
Ref. Libr.
Ohio State University
Columbus, OH 43210

Pepper, Dave
Ref./Orient. Libr.
Woodward Biomedical Library
Vancouver, BC CANADA

Phillips, Phoebe
IMC/Catalog Libr.
Miami University
Oxford, OH 45056

Pickett, Mary Joyce
Ref. Libr.
Augustana College
Rock Island, IL 61201

Piele, Linda
Librarian
University of Wisconsin – Parkside
Kenosha, WI 43151

Pollard, Larry G.
Ref. Libr.
Radford College
Radford, VA 24142

Prince, William
Head -- General Ref. Division
Virginia Polytechnic Institute &
  State University
Blacksburg, VA 24061

Rader, Hannelore
Coor. -- Ed./Psych. Division
Eastern Michigan University
Ypsilanti, MI 48197

Reed, Fred
Publ. Serv. Libr.
St. Clair County Comm. College
Port Huron, MI 48060

Reichel, Mary
Ref. Libr.
UGL--SUNY
Buffalo, NY 14214

Rogers, Sharon
Soc. Sci. Subj. Spec.
University of Toledo
Toledo, OH 43606

Rossi, Gary James
Humanities/Ref. Libr.
Mansfield State College
Mansfield, PA 16933

Rottsolk, Katherine
Ref. Libr.
St. Olaf College
Northfield, MN 55057

Ryken, Jorena
Asst. to the Director
Wheaton College
Wheaton, IL 60187

Sayes, Carol L.
Ref. Libr.
University of Detroit
Detroit, MI 48221

Schobert, Tim
Orient. Librarian
University of Ottawa
Ottawa, Ontario CANADA

Schuckel, Sally
Ref. Libr.
Kellogg Community College
Battle Creek, MI 49016

Schwartz, Vanette
Ref. Libr.
Illinois State University
Normal, IL 61761

Seaman, Sheila L.
Coor. – Publ. Serv.
University of the South
Sewanee, TN 37375

Segal, Jane
Asst. Ref. Libr.
SUNY
Oswego, NY 13126

Seibert, Karen
Ref. Libr.
University of Illinois –
  Chicago Circle
Chicago, IL 60680

Seng, Mary
Head – Spec. Services
University of Texas
Austin, TX 78712

Sharkey, Paulette
Ref./Instr. Libr.
Lansing Community College
Lansing, MI 48901

Simmel, Leslie L.
Head – Ref. Dept.
Bentley College
Waltham, MA 02154

Simon, Rose Anne
LSEP Project Librarian
Guilford College
Greensboro, NC 27410

Smith, Dorman
Tech. Serv.
University of Wisconsin -- Parkside
Kenosha, WI 43151

Snow, Bonnie
Head -- Reader Services
Philad. College of Pharm.
Philadelphia, PA 19104

Somerville, Arleen
Head – Sci./Engin. Libs.
University of Rochester
Rochester, NY 14627

Staffen, Graham
Ref. Libr.
University of Windsor
Windsor, Ontario CANADA
N9B 3P4

Stanger, Keith
Orientation Librarian
Eastern Michigan University
Ypsilanti, MI 48197

Stanton, Vida
Asst. Prof. – Lib. School
University of Wisconsin
Milwaukee, WI 53201

Steffen, Susan Swords
Reader Serv. Libr.
St. Xavier College
Chicago, IL 60655

Strother, Jeanne D.
Lib. Instr. Libr.
Ball State University
Muncie, IN 47306

Surrey, Joan B.
Publ. Serv. Libr.
Rockford College
Rockford, IL 61101

Tracy, Ruth M.
Ref. Libr.
Cornell University
Ithaca, NY 14850

Tran, Thuan
Head Librarian
Western Wisconsin Tech. Inst.
LaCrosse, WI 54601

Traylor, Margaret
Ref. Libr.
College of Alameda
Alameda, CA 94501

Treadway, Cleo
Director
Tusculum College
Greeneville, TN 37743

Van Balen, John
Publ. Serv. Libr.
University of South Dakota
Vermillion, SD 57069

Van Ess, James E.
Ref. Libr.
Carroll College
Waukesha, WI 53186

Vastine, James P.
Assoc. Ref. Libr.
University of South Florida
Tampa, FL 33620

Violette, Judith
Head -- Ref. Dept.
Indiana University--Purdue
  University--Ft. Wayne
Fort Wayne, IN 46805

Vogt, Norman
Head -- General Educ. Lib.
Northern Illinois University
DeKalb, IL 60115

Walker, John T.
Ref. Libr.
Sinclair Community College
Dayton, OH 45402

Wallace, Marjorie
Asst. Lib. Director
Stockton State College
Pomona, NJ 08240

Walter, Jo Ann
Library Technician
Jackson Community College
Jackson, MI 49201

Ward, James E.
Director -- Library
David Lipscomb College
Nashville, TN 37203

Wilt, Lawrence
Asst. Prof. -- Lib. Res.
Dickinson College
Carlisle, PA 17013

Woronoff, Israel
Ed. Psych./Gerontology
Eastern Michigan University
Ypsilanti, MI 48197

Wright, Janie
Ref. Libr.
Southeast Missouri State
  University
Cape Girardeaux, MO 63701